What Your Colleagues Are Saying . . .

"Although the importance of vocabulary knowledge for reading and learning is ~~~~~~~~, it isn't every day that a book makes the connection between word-savvy and engaged text r~~~~~~~~sparent and lively. . . . Laura Robb's *Vocabulary Is Comprehension* is truly a book for the times and for ~~~~~ne-conscious middle grades teacher. It's one I look forward to having in my toolbox."

—**KATHY GANSKE**
Author of *Word Journeys*, Second Edition

"Laura Robb has this remarkable way of lassoing the galloping, impossible-to-meet mandates out there and wrestling them to the ground so they actually work in classrooms. In *Vocabulary Is Comprehension*, she shows teachers how to teach systematic daily vocabulary in the context of authentic reading and a vital curriculum . . . making us grateful once again for Laura Robb and her efforts to help us all be better teachers."

—**JIM BURKE**
Author of *The Common Core Companion*

"The research is clear: the size of a student's vocabulary at the end of twelfth grade is not only a strong indicator of whether college is attainable, but also a predictor of future income and success. Fortunately, *Vocabulary Is Comprehension* provides teachers with effective and practical ideas on how to strengthen our students' knowledge of words. This is an essential book for helping students overcome word deficit and attain the greater freedom and power that comes with possessing a strong and sophisticated vocabulary."

—**KELLY GALLAGHER**
Author of *Deeper Reading*

"Opening Laura Robb's book is like unwrapping a gift box where you discover many other wondrous presents inside. Expertly aligned to the Common Core and to research-based practices, Laura provides teachers with what they've long needed: a simple set of principles for understanding all of the individual *components* of vocabulary along with practical tools for *teaching* vocabulary. . . . Lots of lessons. Lots of texts. Lots of reproducibles. Lots to love!"

—**NANCY BOYLES**
Author of *Closer Reading, Grades 3–6*

"Laura Robb hasn't just shown the best means for employing the most effective instructional strategy for improving word knowledge, she has also thought of every dimension of masterful classroom management to meet the needs of every child along the way. . . . This is a book that will have teachers excited for tomorrow's vocabulary instruction and marveling at how fast students grow in their reading ability when they have tools to employ rather than just rote memorization."

—**JAMES BLASINGAME**
Coauthor of *Teaching Writing in Middle and Secondary Schools*

For Fay Stump, with deep thanks for her support

For my grandchildren, Lucas and Helena

Vocabulary Is COMPREHENSION

Getting to the Root of Text Complexity

Laura Robb

Foreword by Kathy Ganske

FOR INFORMATION:

Corwin

A SAGE Company

2455 Teller Road

Thousand Oaks, California 91320

(800) 233-9936

www.corwin.com

SAGE Publications Ltd.

1 Oliver's Yard

55 City Road

London EC1Y 1SP

United Kingdom

SAGE Publications India Pvt. Ltd.

B 1/I 1 Mohan Cooperative Industrial Area

Mathura Road, New Delhi 110 044

India

SAGE Publications Asia-Pacific Pte. Ltd.

3 Church Street

#10-04 Samsung Hub

Singapore 049483

Publisher: Lisa Luedeke

Development Editor: Wendy Murray

Editorial Development Manager: Julie Nemer

Editorial Assistant: Francesca Dutra Africano

Production Editor: Melanie Birdsall

Copy Editor: Linda Gray

Typesetter: C&M Digitals (P) Ltd.

Proofreader: Susan Schon

Indexer: Wendy Allex

Cover and Interior Designer: Janet Kiesel

Marketing Manager: Maura Sullivan

Photos by Laura Robb.

Printed in the United States of America

Library of Congress Cataloging-in-Publication Data

Robb, Laura.

Vocabulary is comprehension : getting to the root of text complexity/Laura Robb.

pages cm
Includes bibliographical references and index.

ISBN 978-1-4833-4580-2 (pbk.)

1. Vocabulary—Study and teaching.
2. Reading comprehension. I. Title.

LB1574.5.R64 2014
372.44—dc23   2014014058

This book is printed on acid-free paper.

SUSTAINABLE FORESTRY INITIATIVE
Certified Chain of Custody
Promoting Sustainable Forestry
www.sfiprogram.org
SFI-01268
SFI label applies to text stock

14 15 16 17 18 10 9 8 7 6 5 4 3 2 1

Contents

BIG 10

Chapter 3. Figurative Language ... 61

Chapter 4. Getting to the Root of Words ... 109

Chapter 5. General Academic and Domain-Specific Vocabulary ... 130

Chapter 6. Assessing Vocabulary 156

Visit the companion website at
www.corwin.com/vocabularyiscomprehension
for downloadable resources.

Companion Website Resources

Access these resources on the book's companion website at
www.corwin.com/vocabularyiscomprehension

Chapter 2

Reproducible Forms

Understanding Descriptive Words to Visualize

Make and Define Multisyllable Words

Understanding Personification

Write to Show Understanding of Words

Synonyms, Antonyms, and Multiple Meanings

Concept T-Chart

Connotations and Associations

Tweeting to Show Understanding ("The Gettysburg Address")

Four Words

Multiple Forms, Multiple Meanings

Complex Texts

Chapter I, "My Early Home," From *Black Beauty* by Anna Sewell

Excerpt From *Horrible Henry* by Jaime Lockhart

Excerpt From "The Nightingale" by Hans Christian Andersen

"The Nightingale" by Hans Christian Andersen

Excerpt From *Two Regions in Our Solar System* by Lucas Hustick

Excerpt From *Athena and Arachne* retold by Allen Brownwell

Athena and Arachne retold by Allen Brownwell

Excerpt From *Narrative of the Life of Frederick Douglass* by Frederick Douglass

Excerpt From *Narrative of the Life of Frederick Douglass* by Frederick Douglass
(Longer Excerpt)

"The King and the Shirt" by Leo Tolstoy

"The Two Brothers" by Leo Tolstoy

"The Gettysburg Address" by Abraham Lincoln

Sojourner Truth's Speech "Ain't I a Woman?"

Excerpt From "The Canterville Ghost" by Oscar Wilde

Chapter 3

Reproducible Forms

Alliteration ("Three Things to Remember")

Alliteration ("O Wind, Why Do You Never Rest")

Metaphor ("The Highwayman")

Metaphor ("Forecast")

Onomatopoeia ("A Train Went Through a Burial Ground")

Onomatopoeia ("Bedtime")

Repetition ("It's All I Have to Bring Today")

Repetition ("If I Can Stop One Heart From Breaking")

Simile ("Flint")

Chapter 4

Chapter 5

Chapter 6

Additional Resources

Additional Poems for Extra Practice

"The Morns Are Meeker Than They Were" by Emily Dickinson

"The Eagle" by Alfred, Lord Tennyson

Additional Poems for Extra Practice for
English Language Learners and Developing Readers

Repetition

"If I Can Stop One Heart From Breaking" by Emily Dickinson

"Who Has Seen the Wind?" by Christina Rossetti

Alliteration

"O Wind, Why Do You Never Rest" by Christina Rossetti

"Bedtime" by Anina Robb

Idioms and Expressions

"Expressions" by Christina Rossetti

Simile and Metaphor

"Fog" by Carl Sandburg

"Frost" by Anina Robb

"Forecast" by Anina Robb

Denotative and Connotative Meanings

"The Kind Moon" by Sara Teasdale

"How Doth the Little Crocodile" by Lewis Carroll

Complex Texts by Genre

Access these texts on the book's companion website at
www.corwin.com/vocabularyiscomprehension

Poems

Anonymous... "August Heat"

Author unknown, a traditional Anglo-Scottish ballad ...."Lord Randal"

William Blake .... "Three Things to Remember"

Emily Dickinson... "Because I Could Not Stop for Death"

"I Like to See It Lap the Miles"

"If I Can Stop One Heart From Breaking"

"I'll Tell You How the Sun Rose"

"I'm Nobody"

"It's All I Have to Bring Today"

"The Morns Are Meeker Than They Were"

"She Sweeps With Many Colored Brooms"

"There Is No Frigate Like a Book"

"To Make a Prairie"

"A Train Went Through a Burial Ground"

"A Word Is Dead"

John Donne ...."No Man Is an Island"

George Eliot... "Roses"

Ralph Waldo Emerson .... "Concord Hymn"

Eugene Field.. "The Wanderer"

Robert Frost.. "The Road Not Taken"

Johann Wolfgang von Goethe ...."The Erlking"

A. E. Housman... "Loveliest of Trees, the Cherry Now"

Vachel Lindsey .... "The Empty Boats"

Henry Wadsworth Longfellow .... "The Village Blacksmith"

John Masefield .... "Sea Fever"

George Pope Morris... "Woodman, Spare That Tree!"

Alfred Noyes .... "The Highwayman" (first stanza)

Edgar Allan Poe ...."The Raven" (first stanza)

Anina Robb.. "Bedtime"

"Forecast"

"Frost"

Christina Rossetti ...."A Chill"

"A Diamond or a Coal?"

"Expressions"

"Flint"

"O Wind, Why Do You Never Rest"

"Who Has Seen the Wind?"

Carl Sandburg ...."Fog"

William Shakespeare.."Fairy's Song"

"Song of the Witches"

Nonfiction

Fiction

Foreword

In *Vocabulary Is Comprehension: Getting to the Root of Text Complexity,* Laura Robb addresses teachers' need to know about effective vocabulary instruction for middle grades students in the age of Common Core. As a professional who is immersed daily in teaching middle grades students and working with teachers, Laura clearly understands the importance of a systematic yet doable approach for teaching vocabulary.

Although the importance of vocabulary knowledge for reading and learning is widely recognized, it isn't every day that a book makes the connection between word-savvy and engaged text reading so transparent and lively. We know from the research base that understanding lots of words makes it easier to comprehend challenging texts and gain new vocabulary knowledge; conversely, having a limited vocabulary puts learners at risk of reading failure and makes it difficult, if not impossible, for them to acquire knowledge, such as through social studies and science. We also know from decades of research that learners benefit from explicit instruction and meaningful, repeated exposures to the words in different contexts. The new Common Core State Standards has brought the critical role that academic vocabulary plays in learning into sharper focus, and nowhere is this role more vital than in middle and high school. Among other things, the Standards require that students in Grades 4–8 know multiple meanings for words; be able to figure out word meanings by using context clues and Greek and Latin affixes and roots; and determine the meaning of figurative, connotative, and technical language. Young adolescents need to be able to link ideas together using specific words and phrases, such as *by contrast* and *especially;* explain concepts using academic vocabulary; and draw on a variety of language resources. In short, there is much work to be done to develop middle grades students' vocabulary knowledge in the areas laid out by the Standards.

It's clear that Laura Robb is well-versed in the research—and that she is an educator who is in a hurry to make it happen for kids. It's almost as though we can hear her saying, "Okay, gang, enough with all the research and proclamations and handwringing. Like making a soufflé—it's not as hard as it's rumored to be to elevate students' word learning." In a how-to/recipe-like manner that is extremely teacher friendly, Laura presents 10- to 15-minute lessons that integrate vocabulary instruction and the reading of complex texts, mixing in explicit demonstrations, shared reading, collaborative practice, and independent work, activities that tap into the interests of middle grades students. She draws on 10 principles garnered from the Standards to shape the lessons:

1. Promote Meaningful Talk

2. Study Word Parts: Roots, Prefixes, Suffixes

3. Attend to Figurative Language and Connotations

4. Situate Words in Various Contexts

5. Use New Vocabulary in Writing

6. Build Concepts

7. Make Connections

8. Tap Into Technology

9. Promote Independent Reading

10. Deliver Daily Read-Alouds

Goals, a listing of materials (including copies of the short complex texts used in the lessons), practice reproducibles, tips for assisting ELLs, and suggestions for follow-up: It's all right here, enabling busy teachers to dive into teaching without spending a great deal of time collecting materials and planning. Laura describes the lessons in ways that makes them highly accessible, whether for the novice or veteran teacher. Readers will particularly enjoy her conversational writing style, which is peppered with the sort of wisdom and insights (including student reactions) that only a teacher who has taught the lessons can provide. Although practice oriented, the book filters in the whys of current research, including results from national surveys that Laura has conducted with both teachers and students. *Vocabulary Is Comprehension: Getting to the Root of Text Complexity* is truly a book for the times and for the time-conscious middle grades teacher. It's one I look forward to having in my toolbox.

—Kathy Ganske

Acknowledgments

In 1624, the poet John Donne wrote "Meditation 17" that contained this immortal line: "No man is an island." Those words ring true for writing a book, for a book is much more than the author. Think of a concept map, with the writer in the center and branching out from there, teaching colleagues and students, the editor, copy editor, production editor, book designer, and beyond.

I conducted two surveys to inform this book's content, one with teachers and one with students, so I am grateful to hundreds of people who took the time to complete them and give me valuable feedback on the lessons. A special thanks to Elizabeth McDaniel, who contacted teachers she knew in North Carolina, and to Sue Ellis, Stephanie Grieshop, Allison Knowles, Merary Lopez, Sheridan Pagan, and Lori Revel; my sincere thanks for the time you took to do the surveys and collect student surveys.

To the teachers from Westbrook Middle School in Maine, a big "I owe you one" for providing all those surveys: William Brassard, Michael Burke, Paula Curcio, Craig Forrest, Laura Fries, Cheryl Gillespie, Michelle Higgins, Barbara Lloyd, Michael Makin, Robert Moldover, Elizabeth Page, Donna Powell, Cynthia Rice, Stacy Russell, and Stori Shaw. Thanks to Carol Bucci and her dedicated teachers at Colonial Middle School in Pennsylvania.

My deepest gratitude to Fay Stump who invited me to teach many of the lessons to her seventh-grade students in Daniel Morgan Middle School in Winchester, Virginia. Fay's feedback and suggestions strengthened each lesson. My thanks to Robin Northrup and her fifth-grade English language learners, who provided instrumental feedback for lessons on onomatopoeia, simile, and personification. Thanks also to Cheri Kesler, fifth-grade teacher at Powhatan School in Boyce, Virginia, for letting me teach some of the lessons to her class.

To my editor, Wendy Murray—you have a sixth sense for what can make a book sparkle and for providing teachers with lessons that matter and work. I love that the journey of working together continues! To Lisa Luedeke, publisher—thanks for putting Corwin Literacy on the map and recognizing that excellent professional books can be game changers in the lives of teachers and students. To Maura Sullivan, marketing strategist—thanks for your intuitive, informed handle not only on what educators need but on when and how, and for your moxie when it comes to making sure Corwin books are the ones that get talked about in the places that matter. And to Julie Nemer, Francesca Dutra Africano, and the rest of the amazing team at Corwin Literacy—thanks for seeing the book through production and design and attending to all the details that make a book stand out.

Visit Laura Robb's website at www.LRobb.com.

How the Common Core Has Changed the Rules of the Game Forever

(Even If the Standards Go Away)

I wrote *Vocabulary Is Comprehension* to help teachers address the Common Core State Standards' (CCSS) expectations for vocabulary in particular and their emphasis on students' reading complex texts in general. Because here's the thing: If students are going to succeed in reading grade-level literary and informational texts, we are going to need a better game plan in regard to vocabulary instruction. One of the main reasons students are below grade level in their reading proficiency, and struggle to catch up, is their vocabulary deficits (Hart & Risley, 2003b; National Assessment of Educational Progress [NAEP], 2012; Rowe, 2008, 2012; Rowe, Raudenbush, & Goldin-Meadow, 2012).

In this book, I offer that game plan—one that is systematic and yet doable for teachers who are already overloaded with curricular demands. It mirrors the CCSS vocabulary standards and yet also exists on its own, a timeless framework for teaching students how words are built, what they mean, and how to comprehend them in the midst of complex text reading.

At the risk of sounding Pollyannish, excellent vocabulary instruction has the power of closing the big divide between students who do well in school, and in what the CCSS refer to as college and career readiness, and those who don't. Knowing a much bigger bank of words—especially general academic vocabulary—will give a tremendous leg up to our English language learners (ELLs), children living in poverty, and African American and Hispanic students. These capable, smart students may come into school lacking the vocabulary, background knowledge, and experiences necessary for moving from reading two or more years below grade level to reading grade-level complex texts (NAEP, 2011), but that doesn't mean we can't step it up in order to help them progress toward grade level.

And we must. In the 21st century, literacy skills are more essential than ever for success at school and in the workforce. The National Adolescent Literacy Coalition (2007) asserts that the literacy demands that students and teachers face today are 20 times greater than students faced two generations ago. The Common Core vocabulary standards address this urgent issue head on, and that's the way we teachers need to address it.

As you delve into this book and the Common Core vocabulary standards, I encourage you to keep in mind all the English language arts (ELA) standards: reading, writing, speaking, and listening. Really, you can't separate word learning from what it means to *read* complex ideas, to *write* in ways that show ourselves and others what we think and know, to use words we know to *speak* what we know and what we believe, and to use our knowledge of the nuances of language to *listen* closely to others. Word knowledge is at the heart of it all.

Big Ambition: Vocabulary in the Context of All the ELA Standards

The authors of the CCSS point out that "vocabulary instruction has been neither frequent nor systematic in most schools," (National Governors Association Center for Best Practices and the Council of Chief State School Officers [NGAC/CCSSO], 2010, p. 32). This correlates with the results of a survey of teachers I conducted in 2013 (see box below). The Common Core calls for comprehensive and long-term vocabulary instruction in all subjects because vocabulary "has been empirically connected to reading comprehension since at least 1925 (Whipple, 1925) and had its importance to comprehension confirmed in recent years" (NGAC/CCSSO, 2010, p. 32). The Common Core vocabulary standards on pages 3 and 4 stress the importance placed on vocabulary instruction as a pathway to improving reading, thinking, writing, and speaking.

From Sporadic to Systematic

To take the pulse of how teachers currently address vocabulary instruction, I surveyed 300 English language arts and content teachers working in diverse settings in Maine, Ohio, North Carolina, Virginia, and New York.

Vocabulary Questions for ELA and Content Teachers

Please answer these questions in an e-mail.

Provide 3 to 4 sentences for each question.

I will not use your name or your school's name when discussing vocabulary instruction. I might refer to the city and state that you live in.

On page 2 you will find a survey for students to take along with easy-to-complete directions [see Student Vocabulary Survey form at **www.corwin.com/vocabularyiscomprehension**].

Grade and subject you teach: _____

Years of teaching: _____   City and state: _____

1. Do you teach vocabulary before, during, and/or after reading/learning? If so, how?

2. How often do you present vocabulary-building lessons? Can you estimate the length of a lesson?

3. What have you found to be the most effective vocabulary strategies? How can you tell? (For example, you can write "memorizing definitions" or "semantic mapping.") You can also give a brief description if you have no name for it.

4. How does students' knowledge of words influence their comprehension in English language arts? In content subjects?

5. How do you choose words to preteach?

6. Do you follow up with words you preteach during a unit and after the unit? If so what do you ask students to do?

7. Do you teach Greek and Latin roots, prefixes, and suffixes in English language arts? In content subjects?

8. What do you ask students to do with words that come from specific roots?

9. When do you think students should use an online or print dictionary?

10. What would you look for in a book that explains how to teach vocabulary?

The three most consistent responses to the survey were as follows:

1. Teachers recognized that explicit teaching of vocabulary/word study improves reading comprehension.

2. Teachers characterized their vocabulary instruction as sporadic rather than systematic.

3. Teachers cited pressure to prepare students for the state test as a factor in sidelining vocabulary instruction.

The upshot is this: There is a disconnect between knowing that vocabulary is a vital part of student achievement and finding a way to consistently teach it.

Vocabulary in the Context of Complex Text Reading

Take a look at excerpts from the CCSS vocabulary standards for middle grades and middle school, listed below. The recommendations are pretty unimpeachable, right? The standards make clear that for students to comprehend grade-level complex texts, merely learning the definitions of words won't cut it. I admire that they position students' vocabulary acquisition as a multifaceted process and something that occurs through a variety of learning experiences. Teachers can quite easily mine these standards for lesson content and student practice ideas. Indeed, the chapters in this book follow the contours of these standards quite closely.

The CCSS Vocabulary Standards

Standard 4: Determine or clarify the meaning of unknown and multiple-meaning words and phrases based on grade (level) reading and content, choosing flexibly from a range of strategies.

a. Use context as a clue to the meaning of a word or phrases.

b. Use common, grade-appropriate Greek or Latin affixes and roots as clues to the meaning of a word.

c. Consult reference materials (e.g., dictionaries, glossaries, thesauruses), both print and digital, to find the pronunciation of a word or determine or clarify its precise meaning or its part of speech.

d. Verify the preliminary determination of the meaning of a word or phrase (e.g., by checking the inferred meaning in context or in a dictionary).

Standard 5: Demonstrate understanding of figurative language, word relationships, and nuances in word meanings.

a. Interpret figures of speech in context.

b. Use the relationship between particular words to better understand each of the words.

c. Distinguish among connotations (associations) of words with similar denotations (definitions).

Standard 6: Acquire and use accurately grade-appropriate general academic and domain-specific words and phrases; gather vocabulary knowledge when considering a word or phrase important to comprehension or expression.

Supporting English Language Learners and Developing Learners

It's important to differentiate vocabulary instruction for ELLs and developing readers. A wide learning gap exists between ELLs who are newcomers speaking little to no English and those who have been in school for three to five years or more. It's the same with developing readers; a student reading one to two years below grade level has different learning needs than a student reading three to five or more years below grade level.

When planning lessons for either group of students, consider their strengths and how you can build on them. In addition, figure out which parts of a lesson students are ready to receive and work on with you and/or their peers. As you develop lessons that build students' vocabularies, think about designing differentiated experiences that provide success for these students and decide whether you should slow down or speed up the instructional process (Vawter & Costner, 2013).

Differentiation includes *tiering* or offering students tasks appropriate to their reading and speaking expertise (Tomlinson & Cunningham, 2003; Wormeli, 2007). Tiering means that the complexity of a task differs. For example, all students work on roots and affixes, but the teacher asks developing learners to generate fewer words and provides support for figuring out literal definitions. Besides tiering, there are other teaching ideas that advance and support the development of ELL students and developing learners.

On the basis of her case study of an African American immigrant youth, Park (2013–2014) offers recommendations for teaching students with diverse backgrounds:

▶ Provide, before reading, a historical context or overview; discuss the value and relevance of the text; provide some background information on the author.

▶ Choose specific passages that students reread to apply reading strategies and analyze vocabulary once students have the gist of a text.

Developing Readers

Developing readers are students reading three or more years below grade level. They need to build their background knowledge and general academic vocabulary to read grade-level complex texts. I prefer this term because we are all developing readers when tackling texts with unfamiliar content and vocabulary.

▶ Introduce a variety of genres to students and the vocabulary that describes each one.

▶ Build academic literacy by helping students understand the relevance of a text and making personal connections to the text.

Instruction for ELL students and developing readers has to target high-utility words and general academic vocabulary. Lessons should be accessible, relevant, and motivating for students.

Differentiation Tips
Throughout this book, see the recurring "Tips for English Language Learners and Developing Readers." These sections provide ideas for adjusting lessons to students' needs.

Research Highlights

A lack of vocabulary can diminish students' ability to think, speak, read and comprehend, and write about a topic or concept. On the other hand, when students bring a rich and diverse vocabulary to their reading and research, they have the background knowledge to comprehend complex texts in diverse genres (Pearson, 2013). Beck, McKeown, and Kucan (2013), authors of *Bringing Words to Life,* address the relationship between vocabulary and comprehension this way: "There is much evidence—strong correlations, several causal studies, as well as rich theoretical orientations—that shows that vocabulary is tightly related to reading comprehension across the age span in primary grades and with adults" (p. 1). The authors quote from Perfetti and Adolf (2012), "For any encounter with a given test, it is the quality of the reader's word knowledge (form as well as meaning) for the words in that text that is crucial to comprehension" (quoted in Beck et al., 2013, p. 1).

Even though preteaching has gotten some bad press lately in discussions of CCSS, the research shows that preteaching vocabulary is effective. It's been found to play a key part in building students' prior knowledge before reading because words contain concepts and connotative meanings that writers expect readers to have and readers need to read closely and deeply (Marzano, 2004; Pearson, 2013). P. David Pearson (2013) points out that the Common Core's *Revised Publisher's Criteria* "reveals a fundamental misunderstanding of the comprehension process" by asking teachers to keep "prior knowledge at bay" (p. 255). Pearson explains that prior knowledge is not something that readers turn on and off. Not only does prior knowledge of a topic improve comprehension, but also consider that as students read, they continually add to their prior knowledge base.

Catherine E. Snow, professor of education at Harvard Graduate School of Education, calls reading unfamiliar texts with no prior knowledge "cold close reading." Snow (2013) tried cold close reading on an unfamiliar topic. Here's what she says about this experience: "Cold close reading was often unproductive. It was discouraging. I found I couldn't read about the unfamiliar topics for more than a few minutes at a time, and that I was exhausted at the end of such efforts." Moreover, to move beyond the incidental or surface learning of words, students need to meet words many times in reading, listening, and discussions. Preteaching vocabulary starts this process (Beck et al., 2013; Bravo & Cervetti, 2008).

Reading grade-level complex texts means that learners will need a broad knowledge of general academic and domain-specific vocabulary to unpack meaning from these sophisticated materials. Knowing the meanings of words in a text enables students to comprehend main ideas and themes and close read to explore the nuances that connotations and multiple meanings of vocabulary offer. Adams (2009) brings clarity to why vocabulary instruction is the foundation of reading: "Words are not just words. . . . What makes vocabulary valuable and important is not the words themselves so much as the understandings they afford" (p. 180).

The Common Core vocabulary standards recommend that teachers explicitly teach general academic and domain-specific vocabulary and at the same time expand students' vocabularies through the study of roots and affixes, figurative language, and multiple forms of words and their meanings (Beck et al., 2013; Biemiller & Slonim, 2001; Blachowicz & Fisher, 2006; Hiebert, 2005; Hiebert & Lubliner, 2008; Marzano, 2009a; Rasinski, Padak, & Newton, 2008). In addition, Blachowicz and Fisher (2008) point out the importance of intentional vocabulary instruction that includes read-alouds, word play, and word games.

Researchers call for the instruction of general academic vocabulary to boost reading instruction for all learners, especially for ELLs and developing readers who lack the vocabulary to read and comprehend texts in different disciplines (Gottlieb & Ernst-Slavit, 2014; Helman, 2008; Kelley, Lesauz, Kieffer, & Faller, 2010; McKeown, Crosson, Artz, Sandora, & Beck, 2013; Park, 2013–2014).

The Staying Power of the Tiers

It's been more than a decade since researchers Isabel Beck, Margaret McKeown, and Linda Kucan (2002) galvanized our thinking about vocabulary by categorizing words into three tiers, and it continues to be a powerful framework. Their book, *Bringing Words to Life,* is well worth owning, especially if you need a tool for deciding which words to teach. Here is the gist:

- ▶ **Tier One** words comprise 5,500 high-frequency words and rarely require direct instruction, with the exception of ELLs. Most English-speaking students master Tier One words, such as *book, girl, sad, here, there,* and *clock,* through reading and meaningful discussions in Grades K–4.

- ▶ **Tier Two** words comprise 7,000 general academic words that occur across disciplines and are critical to reading comprehension, such as *analyze, evaluate, diminish,* and *profile.*

- ▶ **Tier Three** words comprise 400,000 domain-specific words, such as *peninsula, amino acids, isotope, economics,* and *scientific notation.* They are critical to learning and understanding specific information in the content areas. Domain-specific words are found in informational literature and textbooks.

As you read the rest of this chapter and the chapters that follow, use Beck et al.'s Tier Two and Tier Three words as touchstones for word selection from materials your students are reading. These are the complex, concept-rich words that are worthy of direct teaching so that students gain a depth of understanding about them.

Paying Attention to the National Assessment of Educational Progress (NAEP)

The NAEP's systematic measure of vocabulary began in 2009, forging a tight association between reading comprehension and vocabulary. The premise of this association is that to comprehend complex texts, proficient and advanced readers integrate their knowledge of words' meanings into the context of specific passages in order to understand the topic, themes, and main ideas. The 2011 NAEP results that compared vocabulary performance and reading comprehension showed a strong relationship between word knowledge and reading comprehension. Note, too, that despite the NAEP study that began in 2009, the 2011 results show that we haven't moved the needle enough. There's much work to be done.

> Fourth graders who scored above the 75th percentile in reading comprehension also had the highest average vocabulary score.

> Fourth graders who scored at or below the 25th percentile in reading comprehension had the lowest vocabulary scores.

> In Grade 8 in 2011 and Grade 12 in 2009 (Grade 12 wasn't assessed in 2011), the patterns were similar to fourth graders.

In her webinar for the TextProject & University of California, Santa Cruz, *Growing Students' Capacity With Complex Texts: Information, Exposure, Engagement,* Dr. Elfrieda Hiebert (2013) points out that ideas and concepts are communicated through vocabulary. Hiebert states that "vocabulary is the measure that consistently predicts students' comprehension performance." She goes on to say, "Further: evidence is strong that vocabulary is amenable to instruction" (p. 9).

Though the NAEP scores highlight a lack of improvement in students' vocabulary, Hiebert makes it clear that improving students' vocabulary and closing the vocabulary gap is possible through instruction and a wide range of reading literary and informational texts.

There is a strong relationship between reading comprehension and word knowledge. In order to help students better understand complex texts, we must also improve their vocabulary comprehension.

How the Research Is Distilled Into This Book

There are many, many books on teaching vocabulary to choose from, and many of them are highly effective. What I'd like to think sets *Vocabulary Is Comprehension* apart from the others is that I'm publishing it in this moment in time when the Common Core is galvanizing us to not only get serious about teaching vocabulary but marrying it to complex text reading. With this in mind, I thought about how best to organize a book so that teachers can easily put "it all"—those many important strands of research on vocabulary and comprehension—into their daily instruction. First, the practical solutions I came up with:

- ▶ Extended lessons chunked into 10 to 15 minutes a day that give students interactions with words over 3 to 5 days
- ▶ 50+ brief, complex text or passages right in the book so students are exposed to complex literary and informational texts
- ▶ A lesson structure that ensures student practice
- ▶ Reproducible practice pages students do in class (or at home)

The Lesson Structure: 10 to 15 Minutes a Day

There is a Goldilocks phenomenon to vocabulary professional books: Some are too big (too academic and broad for a teacher to efficiently put to use), some are too small (the 101 lists and games approach that don't provide students with sound word knowledge), and some are just right because they offer a comfortable amount of daily word learning that reflects what we know about best practice. The lesson structure I outline here I think gives a "just right" framework that appeals to teachers and students with its mix of explicit demonstrations, shared reading, collaborative practice, and independent work:

- ▶ **Title:** The title states the lesson focus
- ▶ **Short Complex Text:** Lessons use an excerpt from a literary or informational text to make the connection between word learning and comprehension concrete. Introduce the lesson using the text and then have students practice with texts online (see **www.corwin.com/vocabularyiscomprehension**) and texts they are reading independently
- ▶ **Goals:** States what's to be achieved in the lesson and why it matters
- ▶ **Materials:** What students need; what the teacher needs
- ▶ **Tips for ELLs and Developing Readers:** Ideas for adjusting the lesson to meet these students' needs as well as suggestions for scaffolds
- ▶ **Reproducible:** A one-page sheet of tasks that have students think and write about the lesson's new vocabulary. Students complete it on the last day of the sequence
- ▶ **How I Might Follow Up This Lesson:** Suggestions for supporting all learners once students have completed the lesson

The lesson structure is based on the premise that merely "doing" vocabulary once or twice a week won't cut it. The Common Core vocabulary standards apply to all subjects, and therefore we have to up the ante and offer consistent instruction *across the curriculum*. I believe that if we devote 10 to 15 minutes a day on word learning that relates to general academic vocabulary (Tier Two words) and domain specific vocabulary (Tier Three words), we can make a tremendous difference in students' achievement across the board. Ten to 15 minutes a day can help close the poverty-of-words gap because it provides students with the consistent and comprehensive instruction needed to enlarge academic and domain-specific vocabulary. The remaining chunk of instructional time—a minimum of 30 minutes—is for your curriculum.

Students benefit from one-page reproducible forms that ask them to think and write about new vocabulary after each lesson.

The Big 10 Approach to Reading Words Closely

I knew that beyond a teacher-friendly lesson structure and a nicely succinct time frame, I wanted to devise a concrete method to help teachers execute the lessons in this book—and their own lessons—in a way that honors what we know about literacy *and* what we know about how students best learn. So I developed a list I call "The Big 10," a handful of principles that will help you teach words in a dynamic array of settings. These principles meet each Common Core vocabulary standard and are based in current research on vocabulary. More than anything, The Big 10 help you truly correlate building students' rich vocabularies *while they comprehend complex texts*. And they give you an approach to consistently teaching vocabulary as a way to invest in students' development as readers (Baker, Simmons, & Kame'enui, 1998; Beck, Perfetti, & McKeown, 1982; NAEP, 2011).

#1   Promote Meaningful Talk

Research on early childhood and word learning shouts the importance of talk, listening to others talk, and creating our own oral texts, in learning vocabulary. Clearly, the value of talk at home and in school needs to be reexamined. Meaningful talk is crucial to language development and children's ability to speak, think, understand, read, write, and communicate. One way children learn words is by hearing them used in diverse contexts, by asking adults questions about words to clarify their understanding, and by discussing them with peers and teachers (Beals, 1997; Graves, 2006; Marzano, 2009a; Rosenberg, 2013; Rowe, 2012). In his book, *Choice Words* (Johnston, 2004), researcher Peter Johnston explains, through classroom literacy stories, how what teachers say and the way they say it affects students' thinking; he lists questions and statements that enable students to articulate their ideas in meaningful discussions. Johnston states,

> If we have learned anything from Vygotsky (1978), it is that "children grow into the intellectual life around them." That intellectual life is fundamentally social, and language has a special place in it. Because the intellectual life is social, it is also relational and emotional. (p. 2)

#2   Study Word Parts: Roots, Prefixes, Suffixes

Knowing the meanings of Greek and Latin roots and constructing a set of words related to a root enlarges students' vocabulary and knowledge of word relationships: for example, *inspect, inspector, inspection, inspected, inspecting, introspective*. Rasinski, Padak, and Newton (2008) point out that students learn 1,000 to 4,000 words a year. The study of roots and affixes can enlarge students' vocabulary because they learn eight or more words related to a root and tip word learning closer to 4,000 than to 1,000 words annually (Rasinski et al., 2008). Baumann and Kame'enui point (2004) out that studying roots and affixes is an efficient way for students to learn multiple words related to a root and the words' meanings. Since more than 90 percent of English words of two or more syllables are from Greek and Latin roots, it's crucial to bring this type of word study to all disciplines (Rasinski et al., 2008).

Prefixes change the meanings of words, and knowing their meanings along with the meaning of a specific root can support students' figuring out unfamiliar words while reading. Analyzing word parts is a surefire way to expand vocabulary and observe relationships among words as well as shore up the decoding of multisyllable words

(Bear, Invernizzi, Templeton, & Johnston, 2011; Ganske, 2008; Graves, 2004; Kinsella, Stump, & Feldman, 2003; Rasinski et al., 2008; Robb, 2013).

#3 Attend to Figurative Language and Connotations

Interpreting figurative language and the connotative meanings and associations of words aids students' comprehension of complex texts. Teach students how to use a text to validate their interpretation of figures of speech and to explain the shades of meaning or connotations of specific words in a text.

An understanding of figurative language in a text can help readers visualize an abstract idea by using an example from the real world. Figurative language assists readers with recall and deepens their comprehension of concepts (Giora, 2003; Glucksberg & McGlone, 2001). For example, in *The Great Fire* by Jim Murphy (2010), the author tells readers that in 1871 Chicago was "bound by a combustible knot." The metaphor of a knot, tying things securely together, heightens students' visualization of Chicago as a city with wooden buildings, surrounded by wooden streets and sidewalks, that was ready to ignite.

Bear et al. (2011) in *Words Their Way* suggest how important it is to develop students' sensitivity to words and figurative language because such sensitivity develops readers who can use words, figures of speech, and denotative and connotative meanings to engage with texts, visualize details, and explore layers of meaning.

#4 Situate Words in Various Contexts

Once students have studied and discussed a word, talk about specific situations that a word works in. Knowing situations supports students' writing to show their understanding of a word (Beck et al., 2013; Moore & Moore, 1986; Robb, 2013; Stahl & Nagy, 2006). For example, take a new word, *gargantuan*, meaning huge, very large: A list of situations where gargantuan can be successfully used include describing Godzilla, the Yeti, a spaceship, an airplane, a mountain, an alien creature, an elephant, a skyscraper, and so on.

Providing model sentences that show students how you use a new word and related words in a specific situation can help them craft their own sentences as well as gain additional insights into how a word functions. Sentences can also be used to preteach vocabulary, for with strong context clues, students can figure out the meaning of new words by the way they will be used in the text (Akhavan, 2007; Beck et al., 2013; Moore & Moore, 1986).

#5 Use New Vocabulary in Writing

Students can write using words and pictures to demonstrate their knowledge of words' meanings, of figurative language and connotations, of how words work in diverse situations, and to show relationships and connections between and among words (Beck et al., 2013; Graham & Hebert, 2010). When the English novelist E. M. Forster wrote, "How do I know what I think until I see what I say?" he called our attention to writing as thinking, analysis of ideas, and problem solving.

The litmus test for whether students have absorbed words into their long-term memories is this: Can they think and talk with these words and use them in essays and stories? A goal of comprehensive, long-term vocabulary instruction is for words to become part of students' DNA so they use them to analyze, think, and problem solve on paper.

#6   Build Concepts

Learning words involves more than knowing a definition and how to use a word to show understanding. Effective word learning includes being able to categorize or group words to show the relationship between words and a concept. For example, *instruments* is a concept with diverse categories. One category of instruments relates to the orchestra: percussion, strings, brass, woodwind instruments. These four categories can be subdivided into the kinds of string, percussion, brass, and woodwind found in orchestras. Concept connections can also look at the instruments included in baroque, symphonic, chamber, or jazz orchestras.

Another way to categorize the concept of instrument is to think of specific professions. A surgeon uses instruments: scalpels, lasers, scissors, clamps, staples, needles. A carpenter uses instruments: saw, screwdriver, hammer, nails, levels, pry bar, and so on. The ability to categorize words by concept is complex and should be part of vocabulary learning; analyzing the semantic features or characteristics of words to show how they relate to a concept can deepen and enlarge students' vocabularies (Graves, 2008; Scott & Nagy, 2004).

#7   Make Connections

Connections or associations can help learners remember new words. This strategy is especially helpful for ELLs. Encourage students to make as many connections as they can because these connections will construct deeper understanding and support recall. Take the word *enervating*, meaning to weaken or exhaust. Connections can include noting synonyms—to drain energy—and antonyms—to add energy or strengthen. Students can list things that enervate and connect the new word to their prior knowledge—the flu, running a marathon, extreme heat, dehydration, a high fever—or associate it with a personal experience, such as feeling enervated after taking a long exam (Allen, 1999; Baumann & Kame'enui, 2004; Graves, Juel, & Graves, 1998; Kinsella et al., 2003).

Discussing and understanding denotative and connotative meanings foster connections beyond literal meanings and improve visualization and close reading to explore multiple meanings in a complex text.

Analogies also create connections because each one starts with a comparison, a simile that features a specific relationship and helps learners complete the second part of an analogy (see Chapter 5 for more on analogies).

#8   Tap Into Technology

Since technology is an integral part of students' lives, students should use technology to learn words and their multiple meanings. Using Twitter, blogs, wikis, and interactive computer word games asks students to play with words (Burke, 2012; Gottlieb & Ernst-Slavit, 2014). Playing word games deepens their knowledge of how specific words are used in texts and nudges students to move beyond contextual meanings to understanding words' multiple meanings and relationships. Reference materials that students use will be online dictionaries and thesauri.

#9   Promote Independent Reading

Research shows that students who have rich independent reading lives and read long, diverse texts grow large vocabularies and build extensive background knowledge

(Allington, 2009; Allington & Gabriel, 2012; Allison, 2009; Brozo, Shiel, & Topping, 2008; Cunningham, 2005; Hoyt, 2013a, 2013b; Kamil & Hiebert, 2005; Krashen, 1993; Nagy, Herman, & Anderson, 1985). Independent reading enlarges students' words knowledge as readers repeatedly meet the same words in diverse contexts over long periods of time. When students read, read, read, they fulfill Nagy's (2005) belief that the most effective vocabulary instruction is long-term and comprehensive. Independent readers bump into words dozens of times over months and years. These "word meetings" become comprehensive as students deepen their knowledge of the multiple meanings of words by experiencing how words work.

#10   Deliver Daily Read-Alouds

When teachers read quality literary texts aloud, they tune students' ears to complex syntax and new vocabulary and at the same time build students' listening capacity and background knowledge of a genre and a topic as well as raise their word consciousness (Beck et al., 2013). The next step is to take teacher read-alouds beyond listening and enjoying literary texts to creating interactive read-aloud lessons (see Chapter 2, pages 58–59) that ask students to participate in word-building experiences that can enlarge vocabulary and related concepts and illustrate how figurative language impacts word meaning (Cunningham, 2005; Fisher, Flood, Lapp, & Frey, 2004; Hoyt, 2013a, 2013b; Robb, 2013; Scott & Nagy, 2004).

The Big 10 and the Common Core Vocabulary Standards

The chart that follows lists the Big 10 and the Common Core vocabulary standards that each one addresses. Use the chart to quickly check that you are meeting all the standards as you weave vocabulary instruction into your curriculum.

THE BIG 10	COMMON CORE VOCABULARY STANDARDS
1. Meaningful Talk	4a, 4d, 5a, 5b, 5c, 6
2. Word Parts: Roots, Prefixes, Suffixes	4b, 5b, 5c, 6
3. Figurative Language and Connotations	4d, 5a, 5b, 5c
4. Situations and Sample Sentences	4a, 4c, 4d, 5b, 5c, 6
5. Vocabulary and Writing	4c, 4d, 5a, 5b, 5c, 6
6. Build Concepts	4a, 4b, 4d, 5a, 5b, 5c, 6
7. Connections	4a, 4b, 4c, 4d, 5a, 5b, 5c, 6
8. Technology	4a, 4b, 4c, 4d, 5a, 5b, 5c, 6
9. Independent Reading	4a, 4b, 4d, 5a, 5b, 5c, 6
10. Read-Alouds	5a, 5b, 5c, 6

What's Ahead in This Book

In Chapters 2 through 6, I share lessons and strategies that address the CCSS and these 10 principles; taken together, they will help your students jump the toughest

The Student Survey

Besides surveying teachers, I also conducted a survey of students so I could better understand what tools and classroom formats they felt helped them learn new words (see **www.corwin.com/ vocabularyiscomprehension** for the survey). Eight hundred students in Grades 5 through 8 completed the survey. Ninety percent preferred online dictionaries, and 80 percent agreed that social interactions with peers and being on social media improved their vocabulary. There was 100 percent agreement that learning new words before reading in English, social studies, and science supported comprehension of reading material.

hurdle of complex text reading: challenging words and the challenging ideas they often represent. Here is a glimpse of what's ahead:

▶ **Chapter 2: Ten Short Lessons for the Big 10**—Explores a lesson with a short, complex text and practice reproducible for each one of the Big 10

▶ **Chapter 3: Figurative Language**—Addresses examples of figurative language with definitions, a sample lesson that can be adapted to diverse figures of speech, and poems to use for teaching

▶ **Chapter 4: Getting to the Root of Words**—Uses a 5-day teaching routine to enlarge students' academic and domain-specific vocabulary through a study of Greek and Latin roots, prefixes, and suffixes

▶ **Chapter 5: General Academic and Domain-Specific Vocabulary**—Explores the research on general academic vocabulary and its relationships to students' reading comprehension as well as instructional procedures that work; includes six specific lessons

▶ **Chapter 6: Assessing Vocabulary**—Looks at assessment from the perspective of observing students during the lessons and reading their written work to develop scaffolds and reteach; includes practical tips for making instructional decisions and how to reteach and scaffold

◆◆◆ Collaborate and Learn ◆◆◆

Because I see professional learning and growth as occurring in small, manageable increments, each chapter will close with a short section that invites pairs and/or small groups of teachers and administrators to discuss key points in a chapter. To these conversations, bring examples of what worked in a lesson and what needs adjusting as well as samples of students' work to share and discuss.

1. Why does systematic vocabulary instruction matter? How does the framework support instruction?

2. How do the Big 10 align with the CCSS and research on vocabulary?

3. How will the CCSS for vocabulary affect your instruction? How can you make sure your vocabulary instruction is systematic and comprehensive?

4. Administer the student vocabulary survey (see **www.corwin.com/vocabularyiscomprehension**) and discuss the results. What do the surveys reveal about students' needs? Strengths? Attitudes? Past vocabulary learning? How can you use this information to develop vocabulary lessons and interventions?

Ten Short Lessons for the Big 10

In this chapter, we look at two facets of instruction that apply to all the teaching and learning ideas in Chapters 3 through 6: (a) how to decide which words to teach and (b) how to take the Big 10 principles and lay them out as lessons.

Which Words Do I Teach?

Ah, the siren call of the weekly word list. Wouldn't it be swell if we could just write a list of words and definitions on the chalkboard, have students memorize them, and that would suffice? But as Beck, McKeown, and Kucan (2013) revealed, there are about 7,000 Tier Two words and over 400,000 domain- or subject-specific words, so our weekly list of 10 words falls woefully short. Moreover, checking students' ability to define words has to get beyond the weekly quiz; we want to help students know how to comprehend words while reading and how to use words while speaking, writing, and thinking (Nagy & Hiebert, 2011).

So here's my take: Teach general academic and domain-specific words in the context of your particular curriculum—so the words are relevant to the reading, research, and the diverse writing tasks your students do. If you chase down vast, venerable lists from academic or commercial sources, and try to cover a lot of words, it can backfire. Students can absorb only so much, and they acquire higher-level vocabulary from their independent reading more than from word cramming.

That said, lists of general academic words are available online, and I have included grade-level lists from the Word Up Project, Coxhead's general academic word list, and Jim Burke's list (see **www.corwin.com/vocabularyiscomprehension**). Use these lists as a reference that helps you select specific words in the context of students' studies. Here are some tips that can support your decision about which words to teach:

- Teach words that have poor or no context clues in the text students read.

- Select words that are crucial to an understanding of a unit and texts and teach these before students read.

- Introduce words that are part of directions on tests and writing tasks so students clearly understand your expectations—words such as *evaluate, compare, contrast, define, explain, analyze.*

- Choose general academic vocabulary that relates to topics and texts, and teach for deep understanding as these are the words all readers need to handle complex texts across the curriculum.

Laying Out the Lessons for the Big 10

Use the framework of these model lessons to jump-start your own lesson planning.
Each lesson spans 2 to 4 days, with 10 to 15 minutes devoted to it each day. The lessons will give you a feel for how to orient your vocabulary instruction around these 10 instructional methods that align with Common Core standards. They offer sufficient variety so that attending to vocabulary every day of the school year doesn't go on autopilot. And last but not least, the Big 10 help you make a closer marriage of learning words and reading complex texts.

In subsequent chapters, I go into depth on how to teach figurative language, root words, and so on, but in this chapter what's important is that you and your students experience the short, energetic bursts of these lessons and that you see how, taken together, they provide a variety of experiences for students, from watching you model; to collaborative peer work; to reading, writing, and discussion; and finally to independent reflection.

Elements of the Lesson

Here are some key attributes of the lessons:

- **The words selected support complex text comprehension:** Students will practice and learn general and domain-specific academic vocabulary to help them read the grade-level texts of your curriculum.

- **The lessons encourage student discourse:** The idea here is that the small-group discussion is a rehearsal for writing about words and that when students create oral texts of their understandings it helps reveal to them what they know "rock-solid" and what is still unclear to them.

- **Each lesson has a student reproducible:** See **www.corwin.com/vocab ularyiscomprehension.** You can choose to have students complete the reproducible together, do some for homework, complete it the next day—use these forms as you see fit.

- **Each lesson has extensions ideas:** In sections called "How I Might Follow Up This Lesson" I provide suggestions for extending the lesson and planning short interventions that move students forward with learning vocabulary. *You can extend part of the lesson to another day or complete it on that day using some of your curriculum time.*

- **Each of the lessons is meant as a springboard for you to augment:** These 10 sample lessons provide the bare-bones architecture of what you might do, with the expectation that you notice the basic elements and then create your own. That is, use each one of the Big 10 as springboards to develop your own talk-based lesson prefix and suffix lesson, and so on, using texts that are part of your curriculum.

Be Flexible With Time
Use the 2- to 3-day time frames as ballpark estimates. There may be lessons here you decide to condense into a single day, or you may want to extend one based on your students' needs. For example, when I taught these lessons in Fay Stump's seventh-grade class at Daniel Morgan Middle School in Winchester, Virginia, I noticed that a few English language learners and developing readers needed more than 15 minutes to complete the reproducible, so I added an extra class period to support these students; the rest of the class completed independent reading or written work.

Understanding Descriptive Words to Visualize

 Promote Meaningful Talk

CCSS 4a, 4d, 5a, 5b, 5c, 6

Complex Text:

Excerpt From *Black Beauty* by Anna Sewell, Chapter I, "My Early Home"

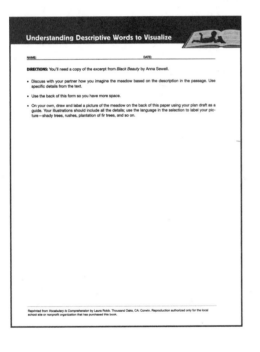

Understanding Descriptive Words to Visualize

NAME: _____ DATE: _____

DIRECTIONS: You'll need a copy of the excerpt from *Black Beauty* by Anna Sewell.

- Discuss with your partner how you imagine the meadow based on the description in the passage. Use specific details from the text.

- Use the back of this form so you have more space.

- On your own, draw and label a picture of the meadow on the back of this paper using your plan draft as a guide. Your illustrations should include all the details; use the language in the selection to label your picture—shady trees, rushes, plantation of fir trees, and so on.

Reprinted from *Vocabulary Is Comprehension* by Laura Robb. Thousand Oaks, CA: Corwin. Reproduction authorized only for the local school site or nonprofit organization that has purchased this book.

> The first place that I can well remember was a large pleasant <u>meadow</u> with a pond of clear water in it. Some shady trees leaned over it, and <u>rushes</u> and <u>water lilies</u> grew at the deep end. Over the hedge on one side we looked into a <u>plowed</u> field, and on the other we looked over a gate at our master's house, which stood by the roadside; at the top of the meadow was a <u>plantation of fir trees</u>, and at the bottom a running brook <u>overhung by a steep bank</u>.

Goals: This lesson uses meaningful talk to help students understand the descriptive words in a text well enough to visualize the setting. The intent is that students apply what they learn in this lesson to their instructional and independent reading so that they become more proficient at honing in on the words that will help them visualize what the author wants them to notice. Beyond seeing settings, descriptive words help readers understand character, conflict between characters, internal and external conflict, and so on. In nonfiction, readers also use visualization to comprehend concepts, quantities, scale, cause and effect, timelines, and so on.

Materials: Copies of the excerpt from *Black Beauty* and the reproducible Understanding Descriptive Words to Visualize for each student (see **www.corwin .com/vocabularyiscomprehension**), chart paper or a whiteboard

▶ Discuss the importance of visualizing, or creating a mental model, in understanding a text. Ask students the following: When do you visualize? How does visualizing help you understand what you read? How can visualizing help you understand vocabulary?

▶ Read aloud the text passage from *Black Beauty*.

▶ Organize students into pairs. Display the phrases and words you've selected: *meadow, rushes, water lilies, plowed, plantation of fir trees, overhung by a steep bank.*

▶ Point to the vocabulary you've displayed. Ask students to read the excerpt from *Black Beauty* twice—first to get the gist or general idea and then to notice the words and phrases and perhaps highlight specific details related to them.

▶ Ask partners to discuss what they know about these words using their background knowledge and context clues. Circulate as students work, assessing their understandings.

▶ Invite each pair to share their ideas, and record students' explanations on chart paper or a whiteboard. You'll have time for just a few comments; continue the following day.

Seventh graders were unsure of the word rushes. *They figured out that it must be a plant because it was with* water lilies *and near the pond. One student explained* plantation of fir trees *as a very large amount of these trees—like huge tobacco fields on a plantation or a plantation of Christmas trees—fields with Christmas trees.*

▶ Finish recording what pairs know about the words and phrases.

▶ Provide a photo or a video clip to deepen understanding.

For example, the seventh-grade teacher projected a photograph of a pond with water lilies and rushes *for students to see. Two boys who had looked up the word* rushes *at night after the first day's lesson said the stems of* rushes *could be woven into mats, ropes, and baskets.*

▶ Ask pairs to discuss how understanding these words and phrases helps them to see what the author is describing.

▶ Have partners create a mental model of the setting based on the excerpt and then share what they imagine with the entire class. Then, using the excerpt from *Black Beauty* as a guide, have students plan, on their own sheet of scratch paper, where they'll place specific items that are in the paragraph.

▶ Have students use their plan to complete a map or drawing of the setting on the back of the reproducible Understanding Descriptive Words to Visualize.

Tips for English Language Learners and Developing Readers

▶ Partner ELL students who have a solid command of English with students whose primary language is English. Students who are at a similar level of strengths/needs with the strategy or are no more than a year apart in reading skill can support one another.

▶ Meet with ELL students who have a limited knowledge of English and provide concrete examples of the words; use online picture dictionaries.

▶ Help students visualize the setting by starting with the meadow and the pond; then ask each student to add an image from the paragraph.

▶ Continue to provide scaffolds while students use the back of the reproducible to illustrate the setting.

How I Might Follow Up This Lesson

▶ If I notice that students need additional strategies for figuring out unknown words, I might present another meaningful talk lesson that began with a brief think-aloud about how I look all around the word for clues. I would use a different excerpt, maybe a nonfiction one that is just as descriptive as *Black Beauty* (see the excerpt from *Twelve Years a Slave* on **www.corwin.com/vocabularyiscomprehension** or use a selection you choose).

▶ I'd ask individual students or pairs to find a passage in a text that contained words and phrases that seemed ripe for visualizing and share it with the class. For students who require extra practice writing their visualization, I could use some of the passages students presented.

Rodrigo's plan is sketchy, but the clarity of his visualization shows in his drawing.

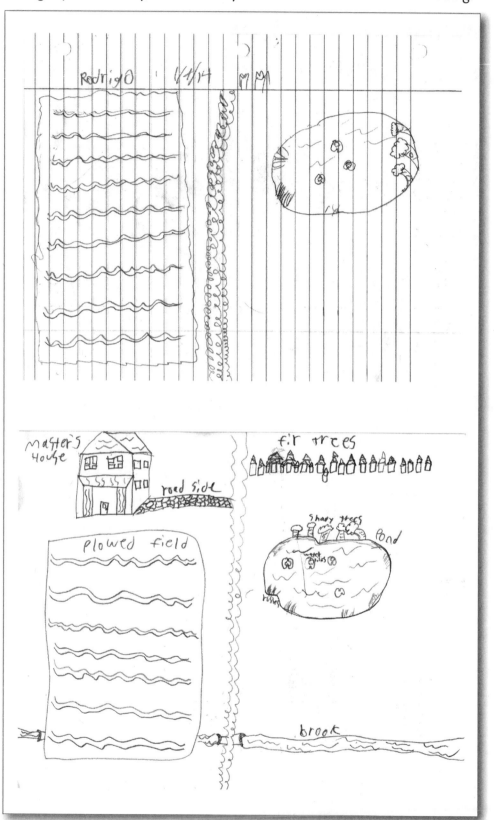

Make and Define Multisyllable Words

 BIG 10 #2 Study Word Parts: Roots, Prefixes, Suffixes

 CCSS 4b, 5b, 5c, 6

Complex Text:

Excerpt From *Horrible Henry* by Jaime Lockhart

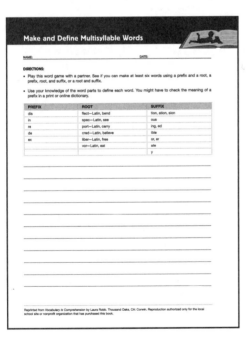

Make and Define Multisyllable Words

NAME: _____ DATE: _____

DIRECTIONS:
• Play this word game with a partner. See if you can make at least six words using a prefix and a root, a prefix, root, and suffix, or a root and suffix.

• Use your knowledge of the word parts to define each word. You might have to check the meaning of a prefix in a print or online dictionary.

PREFIX	ROOT	SUFFIX
dia	flect—Latin, bend	tion, ation, sion
in	spec—Latin, see	ous
re	port—Latin, carry	ing, ed
de	cred—Latin, believe	ible
ex	liber—Latin, free	or, er
	vor—Latin, eat	ate
		y

Reprinted from *Vocabulary Is Comprehension* by Laura Robb. Thousand Oaks, CA: Corwin. Reproduction authorized only for the local school site or nonprofit organization that has purchased this book.

An <u>infamous</u> historical figure, Henry VIII, <u>decapitated</u> his six wives and hundreds of Englishmen during his reign. To divorce his first wife, Catherine of Aragon, a Roman Catholic and his brother's widow, Henry severed England's relations with the Pope and the Vatican, <u>declared</u> himself head of the Church of England and started the English <u>Reformation</u>.

Note: This is an excerpt from an informational text by a student.

Goals: A solid knowledge of Latin and Greek roots, prefixes, and suffixes can help readers decode multisyllable words and figure out their denotative meanings, a valuable aid while reading grade-level, complex texts. In this lesson, students practice a strategy that asks them to look through an entire word and then use their knowledge of word parts to decode or say the word and understand its meaning. Often, once students can say a word, they realize they've heard it and know its meaning. The words in focus are *infamous, decapitated, declared, Reformation.*

Materials: Copies of the *Horrible Henry* excerpt and the reproducible Make and Define Multisyllable Words, readers' notebooks with a section set aside for vocabulary and word building, copies of the two handouts Twenty Most Common Prefixes and Twenty Most Common Suffixes (see **www.corwin.com/ vocabularyiscomprehension**), chart paper or whiteboard

Day 1

▶ Give students a copy of the excerpt from *Horrible Henry* and read the selection out loud.

▶ Discuss the meanings of the prefixes in the featured words: *in* means not, in, into; *de* means removal, away; *re* means again or back.

▶ Explain that suffixes indicate part of speech. Words ending in *tion, ation,* and *sion* are nouns. Words ending in *ous* are adjectives; words ending in *ed* are the past tense of a verb. Write these on chart paper or a whiteboard.

▶ Ask students to pair-share about the prefixes they know. Explain that prefixes are important because they change a word's meaning. Add these to the chart or whiteboard.

Day 2

▶ Model for students how you use word parts to decode a word's pronunciation and meaning. Write the four steps on chart paper or project them onto a whiteboard. Here's what I say for *disconnecting*:

    1. If you see a prefix, write and say it (*dis*).

    2. If you see a suffix, write and say it (*ing*).

    3. Look at what's left—a base word or root—say it (*connect*).

    4. Now put the word parts together: *disconnecting*. This strategy helps students avoid guessing because it asks them to look through the entire word.

▶ Organize students in partners.

▶ Ask partners to use the process to decode: *infamous, decapitated, declared, Reformation.*

▶ Have students share what they did to decode each word.

Readers' Notebooks
Students record their hunches, predictions, emotional reactions, and inferences about reading in readers' notebooks. A notebook can also include a section for vocabulary and word building. Students can use marble covered or spiral bound composition books or handmade notebooks that consist of composition paper stapled between colored construction paper.

Day 3

▶ Give students a copy of the handouts Twenty Most Common Prefixes and Twenty Most Common Suffixes to use as a resource.

▶ Model how you use word parts to define *disconnecting*. Here's what I say:

The prefix *dis* means not; *ing* is a present tense verb ending; the base word *connect* means to join, so disconnecting means not joining.

▶ Organize students into pairs.

▶ Have pairs use their understanding of word parts to define *infamous* and *Reformation* using their prefix and suffix handouts.

▶ Invite partners to share their thinking by giving the word's literal meaning and any connotations they know.

{
One pair of sixth graders pointed out that in *means not, so* infamous *means not famous.*

Another pair added that the connotations of infamous *are negative, more than not famous, like doing evil—kinda like Hannibal Lecter in the movie* The Silence of the Lambs.

For Reformation, *students said it was a movement; that's why it begins with a capital letter.* Re, *a pair said, means back or again—literally it means to form again. In the paragraph it means no more Catholicism and Pope but rather an English church led by Henry VIII.*

Organize students into pairs and have them work together to use their understanding of prefixes and suffixes to define difficult words.

Day 4

▶ Ask students to complete the reproducible Make and Define Multisyllable Words.

Tips for English Language Learners and Developing Readers

▶ ELL and developing readers benefit from knowing word parts. For students reading below grade level, introduce multisyllable words they will meet in a text *before* reading.

▶ Help students use the process modeled in the lesson to decode a word.

▶ Show students the meaning of the prefix and root or base word to help them figure out the word's meaning.

▶ Have students write new prefixes, suffixes, roots, and base words, along with meanings and parts of speech in a section of their readers' notebooks set aside for vocabulary.

▶ Invite students to read the selection and discuss it with them. Encourage students to use their prefix and suffix handouts.

How I Might Follow Up This Lesson

▶ To provide practice with decoding for a group or the entire class, I would have students practice decoding one multisyllable word a day. I'd have students work in pairs, and once they "get it," I'd have them practice independently. Some words you can use are *indigestion, biology, redistribute, rehabilitation, intractable, oversimplification, reposition.*

▶ To help students use word parts to figure out literal meanings, I might ask all students to memorize the meanings of prefixes attached to the words they study. I might also move from decoding a sample word to having students use the word parts to figure out meaning and part of speech.

Understanding Personification

 **Attend to Figurative Language and Connotations**

CCSS 4d, 5a, 5b, 5c

Complex Text:

Excerpt From "The Nightingale" by Hans Christian Andersen

Understanding Personification

NAME: _____ DATE: _____

DIRECTIONS: Rewrite each sentence using personification.

1. Before writing, brainstorm a list of two to three ideas for personifying the item. Think of what a human being says, does, or feels to find a way to personify the mountain and kite.

Dewdrops covered the grass.

Brainstorm: _____
_____
_____

The mountain is high above the city.

Brainstorm: _____
_____
_____

The kite is in the sky.

Brainstorm: _____
_____
_____

2. Choose two words from the list below to personify and use each one in a sentence. Brainstorm a few ideas before writing your sentence.

wind   hurricane   tornado   night   foghorn

The word: _____

My brainstorm: _____
_____

The poor emperor could hardly breathe. He seemed to have a weight on his chest. He opened his eyes and then he saw that it was Death sitting upon his chest, wearing his golden crown. In one hand he held the emperor's golden sword, and in the other his <u>imperial banner</u>. From among the folds of the velvet hangings peered many curious faces. Some were <u>hideous</u>, others gentle and pleasant. They were all of the emperor's good and bad deeds, which now looked him in the face when Death was weighing him down.

Note: See entire story at **www.corwin.com/vocabularyis comprehension**.

Goals: In this lesson, students will understand personification, a type of figurative language that ascribes human qualities (e.g., feelings, speech, behavior, or form) to something that doesn't have these qualities. Students will also grasp how this technique heightens a reader's connection with a text. In addition to understanding personification in texts, it's important for students to understand the role of personification in their writing.

Materials: A copy of the excerpt from "The Nightingale" and the reproducible Understanding Personification for each student (see **www.corwin.com/vocabulary iscomprehension**)

Day 1

▶ Review personification with students who are familiar with this figure of speech.

▶ If personification is new to most students, take 15 minutes to provide students with examples to discuss such as the following:

  ○ A tired Winter limped out, making way for April's soft tears.
  ○ The moon played hide-and-seek with the clouds.
  ○ Laughing and dancing, the waves rolled onto the shore.

Fourth-grade students agreed that having the moon play hide-and-seek helped them visualize the motion of the clouds covering and uncovering the moon. They also said that "hide-and-seek" added a playful, high-energy feeling.

Instead of simply seeing waves roll into shore, one pair explained that "laughing and dancing" raised awareness of the sound of the waves and helped them picture a sunny day and watch the happy motion or dance of the waves.

Day 2

▶ Give students a copy of "The Nightingale" and read it aloud.

▶ Involve students in understanding words they might not know such as *imperial banner* and *hideous*.

The fourth-grade teacher projected onto a whiteboard a definition of imperial *as students did not know this word. Once they read the definition, students linked it to emperor and said it meant a royal banner—the emperor's banner.*

▶ Organize students into groups of four.

▶ Have them read the excerpt for the gist and then reread it closely to notice specific details about Death and the good and bad deeds.

▶ Ask students to discuss how Andersen personifies Death and how he treats the Emperor's good and bad deeds.

Here's what a group of fourth graders said: "Death is a person who sits on the Emperor's chest and wears the crown and who holds the sword and banner. This shows that Death is taking the Emperor's life. Death weighing the Emperor down is Death taking life and breath from his victim. The good and bad deeds of the Emperor's life are personified as faces. This helps you see how ugly or nice each face or deed was."

Herson brainstorms to figure out how he intends to personify objects; then composes sentences.

Understanding Personification

NAME: Herson Andrade   DATE:

DIRECTIONS: Rewrite each sentence using personification.

1. Before writing, brainstorm a list of two to three ideas for personifying the item. Think of what a human being says, does, or feels to find a way to personify the mountain and kite.

Dewdrops covered the grass.

Brainstorm: Bejeweled, sparkle

The mountain is high above the city.

Brainstorm: Stand tall & proud

The kite is in the sky.

Brainstorm: Soaring, flapping

2. Choose two words from the list below to personify and use each one in a sentence. Brainstorm a few ideas before writing your sentence.

(wind)   hurricane   (tornado)   night   foghorn

The word: wind

My brainstorm: Roaring

My sentence: The roaring wind ran across me during the spring.

The word: tornado

My brainstorm: dances does the harlem shake

My sentence: The tornado does a dance called the Harlem Shake over the houses.

3. How does personification create a strong visual picture? Use one of your sentences to explain this.

▶ Ask: How does personification help you visualize? How does it help your understanding?

{
A fourth grader said that personification makes you stop and think about the image. It calls attention to it—like Death—and you remember all the details so you can see Death sitting on the emperor's chest and sucking out the emperor's breath.

Day 3

▶ Have students complete the reproducible Understanding Personification.

▶ If several students struggle with personifying objects in writing, break the process into steps for these students: (1) decide whether you will use feeling, action, or spoken words; (2) think of a situation or context for a personified word.

Tips for English Language Learners and Developing Readers

▶ Support students by giving them several examples of personification and discussing one for the students.

▶ Invite students to discuss the other examples and explain how personification enables them to connect to a nonhuman object.

▶ Help those students who might not be successful working with a partner to complete the reproducible.

How I Might Follow Up This Lesson

▶ To give students more practice with personification, I'd project a poem onto the whiteboard and think aloud to show them how I respond to personification and how understanding the image lets me interpret theme and main idea. I would have pairs work together to discuss a different poem rich in personification and how this moves them deeper into the poem's meaning. (See sample poems rich in personification at **www.corwin.com/vocabularyiscomprehension**.)

▶ I'd ask students to bring in examples of personification from their reading to share and discuss with peers. I might also Google "personification examples"; project these onto a whiteboard, and ask pairs to choose two to discuss and then share their interpretations with the class.

Write to Show Understanding of Words

 Situate Words in Various Contexts

CCSS 4a, 4d, 5a, 5b, 5c, 6

Complex Text:

Excerpts From *Two Regions in Our Solar System* by Lucas Hustick

Our <u>solar system</u> is vast and part of a galaxy known as the Milky Way. The solar system includes the sun and all the objects that travel around the sun, a medium sized star: <u>planets</u>, the moon, the <u>asteroid belt</u>, comets, meteoroids, and man-made satellites that circle the Moon and Mars.

<u>Scientists</u> <u>divide</u> the planets in our solar system into two groups—the inner planets and the outer planets. The inner planets are the four closest to the sun: Mercury, Venus, Earth, and Mars. The outer planets are Jupiter, Saturn, Uranus, and Neptune. An asteroid belt that contains thousands of <u>rocky</u> objects smaller than planets, located

(Continued)

Write to Show an Understanding of Words

NAME: _____ DATE: _____

DIRECTIONS:

- Write sentences on separate paper headed with your name and date.
- Write a sentence that shows understanding of five words you choose from the words listed below.
- Use the situations on the chart to help you write a sentence that shows understanding of the word.

WORD	SITUATIONS
solar system	the sun, any of the planets, gravity
regions	areas on earth, areas in space
rocky	places with rocks—planets, mountains, space rocks, or asteroids
asteroid belt	space rocks, largest number of asteroids are between Mars and Jupiter, have no atmosphere so can't have life, can be all through solar system
planets	large round object in space that travel around a star like the sun; eight planets in our solar system
terrestrial	relating to the earth; living and growing on land—terrestrial plants, animals, humans, birds, habits of earthbound creatures
divide	numbers, food such as pizza or cake, students into groups, money
scientists	people who study biology, botany, geology, chemistry, physics, teachers of science, books and movies about scientists

Reprinted from *Vocabulary Is Comprehension* by Laura Robb. Thousand Oaks, CA: Corwin. Reproduction authorized only for the local school site or nonprofit organization that has purchased this book.

(Continued)

between the orbits of Mars and Jupiter, separates the inner and outer <u>regions</u>.

Planets in the inner and outer regions have different characteristics. The four inner planets, called <u>terrestrial</u> planets, have solid surfaces similar to our Earth. The four outer planets, called gas giants, have no solid surfaces and are gaseous planets.

Note: This is an excerpt from an essay by a student.

Goals: It's easy for students to memorize a definition of a word. However, definition alone does not indicate comprehension of a word. This lesson will help students write sentences that illustrate their understanding of words by having students and the teacher suggest situations for specific words. The selected words are *solar system, planets, asteroid belt, scientists, divide, rocky, regions, and terrestrial.*

Materials: Copies of the excerpt from *Two Regions in Our Solar System* and the reproducible Write to Show Understanding of Words for each student (see **www .corwin.com/vocabularyiscomprehension**), chart paper or whiteboard

---

Day 1

▶ Before reading, ask students which words they understand, using their prior knowledge: *solar system, regions, rocky, asteroid belt, terrestrial, planets, divide,* and *scientists.* Have students share their understandings with the class.

▶ Close read the excerpt with students to build their prior knowledge and understanding.

▶ Based on students' input, decide which words you need to preteach and have students discuss.

▶ Preteach using pictures, photographs, and online videos.

Day 2

▶ Organize students into pairs.

▶ Have students help you complete a chart by suggesting situations for writing about the listed words (see example below).

▶ Have pairs discuss and share their situations. As the teacher, you can add situations once students' stop offering suggestions.

▶ Write one to three sample sentences, thinking aloud to make your process visible. Show students how the situation helps you compose a sentence that illustrates an understanding of the word. Such a lesson expands students' mental model of using specific words and stirs discussions and questions that enlarge their knowledge base. Here's what I say and write for *terrestrial*:

> A situation I can write about for terrestrial is to refer to types of plants and animals that live in a specific region of the earth. I think I'll write about the desert and cacti and lizards.

▶ Here's what I write:

> A common <u>terrestrial</u> plant and reptile that you'll find on the desert are cacti and darting lizards.

One seventh grader asks, "What about extraterrestrial—like E.T.?"

"What does it mean?" I ask.

"Another student says, extra means beyond or outside of, so extraterrestrial is something that lives outside of the earth on a different planet or galaxy."

"Can I give a sentence?" asks a third student. I nod. Here's what she offers: "E.T. is an extraterrestrial that came to earth from Brodo, a planet that doesn't exist."

▶ Encourage students' questions, and you'll build their engagement and vocabulary.

Word	Situations
solar system	the sun, any of the planets, gravity
planets	large round object in space that travel around a star like the sun; eight planets in our solar system
asteroid belt	space rocks, largest number of asteroids are between Mars and Jupiter, have no atmosphere so can't have life, can be all through solar system
scientists	people who study biology, botany, geology, chemistry, physics, teachers of science, books and movies about scientists
divide	numbers, food such as pizza or cake, students into groups, money
rocky	places with rocks—planets, mountains, space rocks or asteroids
regions	areas on earth, areas in space
terrestrial	relating to the earth; living and growing on land—terrestrial plants, animals, humans, birds, habits of earthbound creatures

A chart students and I created in class.

Day 3

▶ Have students complete the reproducible Write to Show Understanding of Words.

Tips for English Language Learners and Developing Readers

▶ Show photographs and videos to enlarge students' understanding of the words.

▶ Help this group choose words they can successfully use in a sentence.

▶ Suggest that students with less expertise with English choose 2 to 3 words.

▶ Gather the group that needs your support and work with them.

How I Might Follow Up This Lesson

▶ To help students see the importance of knowing situations that words work in because the situation provides the context for a word, I would use a different text, and together, we would find situations for specific words. Then I would model how I compose a sentence using one of the words and a specific situation. If students are ready to work with a partner, I'd have them write a sentence for the other words.

▶ Next, I'd ask partners to share their sentences with the group. By giving students multiple models and opportunities to observe others' composing process, you can expand their mental model and move them to independence.

Synonyms, Antonyms, and Multiple Meanings

BIG 10 #5 Use New Vocabulary in Writing

CCSS 4c, 4d, 5a, 5b, 5c, 6

Complex Text:

Excerpt From *Athena and Arachne* retold by Allen Brownwell

Athena was Zeus's daughter. She was his favorite child and born in a most <u>unusual</u> way. After learning that his wife Metis would one day bear a son who would kill him, Zeus decided to trick Metis. He started a <u>shape-shifting</u> game with her, and when he challenged her to turn into a fly, she <u>obliged</u>—and he quickly swallowed her up. Metis did not take kindly to this and prepared to welcome her daughter by fashioning a robe and a helmet. The hammering inside his head <u>agonized</u> Zeus, and he begged Hephaestus to help him. The <u>skilled</u> smith opened Zeus's skull without harming him, and out sprang bright-eyed Athena. Goddess of wisdom and

(Continued)

Synonyms, Antonyms, Multiple Meanings

NAME: _____ DATE: _____

DIRECTIONS:

- Discuss the words with a partner and think of synonyms and antonyms.
- Complete the chart below by providing two synonyms and two antonyms for each word and two situations the word could be used in. You can use an online dictionary to check and adjust your work.
- Choose three words and use the word and a situation in a sentence to show you understand its meaning.

SYNONYM-ANTONYM CHART

WORD	SYNONYMS	ANTONYMS	SITUATIONS
	1.	1.	1.
	2.	2.	2.
	1.	1.	1.
	2.	2.	2.
	1.	1.	1.
	2.	2.	2.
	1.	1.	1.
	2.	2.	2.
	1.	1.	1.
	2.	2.	2.

> **(Continued)**
>
> skill, she was a fierce warrior and loyal protector of brave heroes. Yet she <u>excelled</u> in the <u>domestic</u> arts as well; she was a master weaver and created beautiful embroidery. Proud and strong, Athena was a powerful force among the gods.
>
> *Note:* See entire myth at **www.corwin.com/vocabularyiscomprehension**.

Goals: Knowing synonyms and antonyms broadens students' knowledge of words and prepares them for standardized tests. The ability to generate synonyms and antonyms indicates students' understanding of a word's meaning and allows them to move into using the word in a sentence with ease. To help students use their knowledge of a word's meaning to find synonyms and antonyms, this lesson uses an excerpt from *Athene and Arachne*. First students must use the context and their prior knowledge to deepen their knowledge of a word's meaning. They then work in pairs to find synonyms and antonyms, find situations the word can be used in, and then write sentences that illustrate their understanding of the word. The selected words are *unusual, shape-shifting, obliged, agonized, skilled, excelled,* and *domestic.*

Materials: Copies of the excerpt from *Athene and Arachne* and the reproducible Synonyms, Antonyms, and Multiple Meanings for each student; readers' notebooks; teaching chart (see **www.corwin.com/vocabularyiscomprehension**), chart paper and whiteboard

---

Day 1

- Before reading aloud this excerpt, give a brief background on the Greek Gods, pointing out that Athene was the goddess of wisdom, just warfare, and the domestic arts. You might also explain that spiders, or arachnids, are named for Arachne.

- Review the meaning of *synonym* and *antonym* and provide concrete examples for students. For example, I use the word *skill* from *Athene and Arachne*. Sixth-grade students offered these synonyms—*ability, talent, expertise*—as well as these antonyms—*incapable, incompetent, inability*.

- Give students a copy of *Athene and Arachne* and read it out loud.

- Ask students to read the selection once to get the gist and a second time to try to use context clues to figure out the meanings of the underlined words.

- Model how you use context clues to figure out a word's meaning. Here's what I say:

  > I'm trying to figure out the meaning of *unusual* in this sentence: *She was his favorite child and born in a most unusual way.* I can think of the way she was born when I read for the gist and figure out that unusual means different. I know that the prefix *un* means "not" so she was born in a way that was not usual or normal. Now I can find synonyms: *different, unique, strange, noteworthy, abnormal*. Once I know the meaning and synonyms, I can identify antonyms: *normal, ordinary, regular, expected, pedestrian*.

- Ask pairs to think of situations in which they could use *unusual* in a sentence to show an understanding of its meaning. Students suggested a costume party, gift, hairstyle, and pet.

▶ I write this sentence using the situation of a costume party:

> Dressed as an iguana for his class's costume party, Carlos won the prize for most <u>unusual</u> and realistic costume.

▶ Organize students into pairs.

▶ Ask pairs to use clues in the paragraph and sentence to figure out the meaning of *agonized*. Pairs share their ideas with the class. One pair explained *agonized* as intense or extreme pain.

▶ Have pairs think of two synonyms and two antonyms and share their suggestions with the class. Two synonyms that sixth-grade students offered are *tortured* and *tormented*; two antonyms are *comforted* and *soothed*.

▶ Invite pairs to suggest situations for *agonized* and then use one in a sentence that illustrates understanding. A pair offered these situations for agonized: a toothache, stitches without painkiller, a broken arm or leg, a deep cut.

Here are two sentences they wrote:

1. *The doctor quickly stitched the large forehead cut and <u>agonized</u> Paolo because there was not time for a painkiller.*

2. *The toothache <u>agonized</u> Justin making his cheek swell and head throb so he could think of nothing but pain.*

▶ Have students complete the reproducible Synonyms, Antonyms, and Multiple Meanings.

Tips for English Language Learners and Developing Readers

▶ Read aloud the selection to students or give them a different, more accessible selection to work with.

▶ Build in more practice using context to figure out words' meanings from the selection and then identifying synonyms, antonyms, and situations.

▶ Share synonyms, antonyms, and situations with students and have them discuss the situations and how they might use the word in a sentence.

▶ Ask students who can find synonyms and antonyms to find one of each.

▶ Support these students as they complete the chart of the reproducible.

How I Might Follow Up This Lesson

▶ For students who seem tentative with the concept of antonyms and synonyms, I would work with them using words whose definitions they understood. And then I'd ask them to use their background knowledge to find antonyms and synonyms.

▶ I might have students explore antonyms and synonyms for a word using an online dictionary as long as the students had a solid understanding of the word's meaning.

▶ For additional practice with finding situations, I would help students generate situations for the antonyms and synonyms they identified for a specific word and then ask students to choose two to four to use in sentences.

Neysha shows her understanding of words by thinking of synonyms and antonyms.

Synonyms, Antonyms, Multiple Meanings

NAME: *Neysha Washington*   DATE:

DIRECTIONS:

- Discuss the words with a partner and think of synonyms and antonyms.

- Complete the chart below by providing two synonyms and two antonyms for each word and two situations the word could be used in. You can use an online dictionary to check and adjust your work.

- Choose three words and use the word and a situation in a sentence to show you understand its meaning.

SYNONYM-ANTONYM CHART

WORD	SYNONYMS	ANTONYMS	SITUATIONS
Shape shifting	1. Change, new 2.	1. Stay the same 2. normal	1. Gymnastics 2.
Obliged	1. agree, accept 2.	1. disagree 2. disaprove	1. Meeting 2. Debate
Skilled	1. Talented 2. expert	1. untalented 2.	1. social studies 2.
excelled	1. achive 2.	1. Poorly 2.	1. Goal 2.
domestic	1. not wild 2.	1. wild crazy 2.	1. Tame animals 2.

The Gymnast is shapeshifting because, she is changing her body positions. I was obliged to follow the rules. I am skilled in social studies. I have excelled in my reading this year. Goats are domestic animals.

Seventh-grade English teacher Fay Stump uses the strategy with "Rikki-Tikki-Tavi."

Synonyms, Antonyms, Multiple Meanings

NAME: Nico   DATE:

DIRECTIONS:

- Discuss the words with a partner and think of synonyms and antonyms.

- Complete the chart below by providing two synonyms and two antonyms for each word and two situations the word could be used in. You can use an online dictionary to check and adjust your work.

- Choose three words and use the word and a situation in a sentence to show you understand its meaning.

SYNONYM-ANTONYM CHART

WORD	SYNONYMS	ANTONYMS	SITUATIONS
Valiant	1. Brave 2. Courageous	1. Cowardly 2. Scared	1. fight with Dragon 2. Roler Coaster
cunningly	1. Smart 2. clever	1. Dumb 2. Stupid	1. chess 2. hide-n-seek
gait	1. Walk 2. Sway	1. cat Walk 2. run	1. Dancing while waking 2.
Consolation	1. Comfort 2. Fea	1. Sad 2. Deppressed	1. friend 2. Councilar
revive	1. resurect 2. come back	1. Die 2. Death	1. Zombie 2.

The fledgling flew out of the tree.
The fire singed his hair.
Superman valiantly destroyed the villan.
The kids got consolation from friends when their parent died.

Connecting Words to a Text's Concepts

BIG 10 #6 Build Concepts

CCSS 4a, 4b, 4d, 5a, 5b, 5c, 6

Complex Text:

Excerpt From *Narrative of the Life of Frederick Douglass* by Frederick Douglass

Concept T-Chart

NAME: _____ DATE: _____

DIRECTIONS:

- Think of four words or short phrases that come to your mind when you think of "slavery."
- In the first column of the chart, write the word or phrase.
- In the second column, explain how the word or phrase connects to slavery.

WORD OR PHRASE	CONNECTION TO "SLAVERY"
1.	
2.	
3.	
4.	

Reprinted from *Vocabulary Is Comprehension* by Laura Robb. Thousand Oaks, CA: Corwin. Reproduction authorized only for the local school site or nonprofit organization that has purchased this book.

If at any one time of my life more than another I was made to drink the bitterest dregs of slavery, that time was during the first six months of my stay with Mr. Covey. We were worked in all weathers. It was never too hot or too cold; it could never rain, blow, hail, or snow, too hard for us to work in the field. Work, work, work, was scarcely more the order of the day than of the night. The longest days were too short for him, and the shortest nights too long for him. I was somewhat unmanageable when I first went there, but a few months of this discipline tamed me. Mr. Covey succeeded in breaking me. I was broken in body, soul, and spirit. My natural elasticity was crushed, my intellect <u>languished</u>, the <u>disposition</u> to read departed; the cheerful spark that <u>lingered</u> about my eye died; the dark night of slavery closed in upon me; and behold a man transformed into a brute!

Note: See a longer excerpt of this narrative memoir at **www.corwin.com/vocabulary iscomprehension**

Goals: The benefit of this vocabulary exercise is having students think through the connections between a word or phrase and the concept. By making connections, students can deepen their understanding of words in a text as well as related words they suggest. By sharing connections, students provide peers with snippets of stories and experiences that can support recall and a clearer understanding of a word or phrase. The selected words are *languished, disposition,* and *lingered.*

Materials: Copies of excerpt from *Narrative of the Life of Frederick Douglass* and the reproducible Concept T-Chart for each student (see **www.corwin.com/ vocabularyiscomprehension**), chart paper or a computer and whiteboard

---

Day 1

▸ Give students the excerpt from *Narrative of the Life of Frederick Douglass* and read it out loud.

▸ Ask students to identify words they don't understand.

▸ Have students read the sentence that contains each tough word and use context clues to figure out the word's meaning. In some cases, students might have to read the sentence that comes before or after the word to determine meaning. Having students do this prior to reading the selection on their own can help you decide whether the text is too difficult for them. If students need a more accessible text, choose one from online or your class library.

▸ Skip this lesson if students are advanced readers and understand the vocabulary.

Day 2

▸ Have students turn to a partner and discuss what slavery means to them. Record students' ideas on chart paper or in a computer that projects onto a whiteboard.

Here's what eighth graders suggested: "no rights, property, can't make decisions, controlled by a master, often abused and tortured."

▸ Write the words you selected on the chalkboard, chart paper, or a whiteboard. I write *languished, disposition, lingered.*

▸ Organize students into pairs.

▶ Help students say the words and ask them if they think they know anything about each word.

▶ Write an accessible sentence for each word that uses the word the way the text uses it.

▶ Have students use each sentence to figure out the word's meanings.

▶ Here are the three sentences I post:

My muscles languished because I could not exercise.

Because I missed so much school, the disposition to study for the unit test was not there.

The odor of pot roast cooking lingered in the kitchen and dining room.

▶ Invite pairs to share with classmates what they learned about each word.

Day 3

▶ Give students the excerpt from *Narrative of the Life of Frederick Douglass* and read it out loud.

▶ Ask students to read the selection once to get the gist and a second time to recall details of Douglass's life as a slave.

▶ Tell students that the class will start a T-chart about the concept of *slavery*.

▶ Explain to students that they can find words and phrases about slavery in the selection, and they can offer other words and phrases that relate to slavery from their experiences.

▶ Provide a model for students. Here's what I say for *bitterest dregs*:

Dregs can be coffee grinds or tea leaves at the bottom of a cup. They can also be bits and pieces at the bottom of a bottle of wine. This connects to slavery because Douglass's master, Mr. Covey, made him feel the bitter part of being a slave—whippings, long days of work, not enough time to eat.

▶ Invite pairs to use text details to connect *tamed* and *discipline* to the concept of slavery. Here's what students said:

| tamed | Made Douglass listen—tamed implies taking a spirited person and training them to listen to orders |
| discipline | Owners disciplined or made slaves obey by beating them, depriving them of food and sleep, and making them work day and night. |

Eighth-grade students connect words to concept of slavery

Day 4

▶ Ask students to complete the reproducible Concept T-Chart.

Tips for English Language Learners and Developing Readers

▶ Organize students into groups of three.

▶ Find an alternate text if the selection is at students' frustration level.

▶ Read the selection out loud for ELL students and developing readers who can then read the selection independently.

▶ Ask students to identify words that are unfamiliar and discuss these with students.

▶ Work one-to-one with students and help them generate a list of words for the reproducible.

How I Might Follow Up This Lesson

▶ If students have difficulty connecting words to the concept of slavery, I'd review the meaning of slavery and think aloud to show how I use what I know about slavery to connect a word or phrase to it.

To help ELL students and developing readers, organize students into groups of three and ask them to discuss any words from the text they are unfamiliar with.

Understanding Denotative and Connotative Meanings

BIG 10 #7 Make Connections

CCSS 4a, 4b, 4c, 4d, 5a, 5b, 5c, 6

Complex Text:

"The King and the Shirt" by Leo Tolstoy

Connotations and Associations

NAME: _____ DATE: _____

DIRECTIONS:
• Read the excerpt from "The King and the Shirt" by Leo Tolstoy.
• Write the denotative meaning of each word in the chart below.
• Next, write the connotative meaning of each word. You may use an online or print dictionary to help you.

WORD	DENOTATIVE MEANING	CONNOTATIVE MEANING
kingdom		
cure		
poverty		
rich		

Choose one word and explain how understanding its connotations deepened your understanding of Tolstoy's "The King and the Shirt."

_____

_____

_____

_____

Reprinted from *Vocabulary Is Comprehension* by Laura Robb. Thousand Oaks, CA: Corwin. Reproduction authorized only for the local school site or nonprofit organization that has purchased this book.

A king once fell ill. "I will give half my kingdom to the man who can cure me," he said.

All his wise men gathered together to decide how the king could be cured. But no one knew. Only one of the wise men said what he thought would cure the king. "If you can find a happy man, take his shirt, put it on the king—and the king will be cured."

The king sent his <u>emissaries</u> to search for a happy man. They traveled far and wide throughout his whole kingdom, but they could not find a happy man. There was no one who was completely satisfied: if a man was rich, he was ailing; if he was healthy, he was poor; if he was rich and healthy, he had a bad wife; or if he had children they were bad—everyone had something to complain of.

Late one night, the king's son was passing by a poor <u>hut</u> and he heard someone speak: "God be praised. I have finished my work. I have eaten my fill, and I can lie down and <u>sleep</u>! What more could I want?"

The king's son ordered that the man's shirt be taken and carried to the king. "Give the man as much money as he wants," said the king's son.

The emissaries walked into the hut to take off the man's shirt, but the happy man was so poor that he had no shirt.

Goals: The Common Core asks students to understand the denotative and connotative meanings of words so that students understand that words have a literal or denotative meaning and connotative meanings or multiple associations. Knowing these connotations or associations can deepen students' understanding of a complex text by helping them create strong mental pictures. In this lesson, students will discuss the denotative meanings of words as well as words' multiple connotative meanings. This lesson is challenging for students and worthy of repeating with different texts. The selected words are *emissaries, hut,* and *sleep.*

Materials: Copies of the excerpt from "The King and the Shirt" and the reproducible Connotations and Associations for each student (see **www.corwin.com/vocabularyiscomprehension**); access to online or print dictionaries (see another Tolstoy folk tale, "The Two Brothers," at **www.corwin.com/vocabularyiscomprehension**), chart paper and whiteboard

---

Day 1

▸ Review denotative and connotative meanings of words from the excerpt if necessary (students won't read the excerpt until Day 2).

▸ Share the examples in the chart on page 46 with students and have them discuss the mental images that connotations create. These words aren't in the Tolstoy text but are accessible examples of connotation-rich words.

Day 2

▸ Tell students that Leo Tolstoy was a famous Russian writer who wrote *Anna Karenina* and *War and Peace,* two novels that have been made into movies. "The King and the Shirt" is from a collection of short folk and fairy tales he wrote.

▸ Give students a copy of "The King and the Shirt" and read it aloud.

A review of denotative and connotative meanings of words

Word	Denotative Meaning	Connotations
sizzle	to make a hissing sound like frying fat	to seethe with anger; to be very hot as a sizzling summer day; the crackling of popcorn
flexible	capable of bending	branches bending in the wind; flexible muscles from exercising; an agenda; personality trait; no preconceived notions

▶ Think aloud to show students how you figure out the denotative and connotative meanings of *emissaries*. Here's what I say:

> The literal meaning of emissaries is a person or persons sent on a special mission for a government or organization. Examples of connotations or associations include the following: spies sent to gain information from the enemy, danger, disguises, and fear are connotations; an ambassador to a foreign country, assimilating into a culture is a connotation; a representative as the person representing teachers at a union meeting, taking action, voting, and speaking out are connotations; a missionary can be an emissary for a religion.

▶ Invite students to check an online or print dictionary to explore meanings of emissaries. Here's what sixth-grade students offered: a secret agent, an ambassador, a representative.

▶ Organize students into pairs.

▶ Ask pairs to provide the denotative meanings for *hut* and *sleep* as well as the connotative meanings. Here's what students said:

Sixth graders' suggestions for denotative and connotative meanings.

Word	Denotative Meaning	Connotations
hut	A small, simple, one-room house; a shack	dwelling for poor person; place where a person might go to meditate or get closer to God; shelter for hikers and skiers
sleep	resting of body and mind with eyes closed	hibernation; tingling sensation as foot falling asleep; to end a pet's life as in putting it to sleep; death; plants closing petals at night; inactive due to illness or pain of body and mind; sleepover with friends

▶ Invite partners to share what they learned with the class.

▶ Have students complete the reproducible Connotations and Associations.

Tips for English Language Learners and Developing Readers

▶ Support ELL students and developing readers when searching for connotations for *hut* and *sleep* as this will be a challenge for them. Use questions to move them into associations. For example, for *hut* you can ask the following:

- ○ How would you describe the lifestyle of people who live in a hut?
- ○ Why is the building called a hut?
- ○ How would you describe the room inside a hut?
- ○ What defects might a hut have?

▶ Ask these possible questions for sleep:

- ○ When do people sleep?
- ○ Who else besides people sleeps?
- ○ Are there different kinds of sleep?
- ○ Why is sleep important?

▶ Help students complete the reproducible and release responsibility to them once you observe they can work independently.

How I Might Follow Up This Lesson

▶ Since words' connotations are important to understanding complex texts, I might work on connotative meanings and how these affect interpretation of a text. I would do this when working on instructional reading with small groups and use their texts to explore the relationship between connotations and theme and main ideas.

▶ For students who have difficulty with connotations because of a lack of experience and background knowledge, I would use short poems to help them understand how connotations can deepen understanding (see poems at **www .corwin.com/vocabularyiscomprehension**).

Natalie uses connotations to understand the theme of "The King and the Shirt."

Connotations and Associations

NAME: Natalie McGeachy   DATE:

DIRECTIONS:

- Read the excerpt from "The King and the Shirt" by Leo Tolstoy.

- Write the denotative meaning of each word in the chart below.

- Next, write the connotative meaning of each word. You may use an online or print dictionary to help you.

WORD	DENOTATIVE MEANING	CONNOTATIVE MEANING
kingdom	a section of land where a King rules	Poor, rich, controlled, work, presents
cure	some thing that can make a sick person better	new, better
poverty	People who have nothing	poor, nothing
rich	People that recieve higher wages	wealthy, bratty, snotty, greedy

Choose one word and explain how understanding its connotations deepened your understanding of Tolstoy's "The King and the Shirt."

Poverty

The guy is happy with his life. He doesn't care that he has nothing

Showing Word Knowledge via Twitter

 Tap Into Technology

CCSS 4a, 4b, 4c, 4d, 5a, 5b, 5c, 6

Complex Text:

"The Gettysburg Address" by Abraham Lincoln

Fourscore and seven years ago our fathers brought forth on this continent a new nation, conceived in liberty and <u>dedicated</u> to the <u>proposition</u> that all men are created equal.

Now we are engaged in a great civil war, testing whether that nation or any nation so conceived and so dedicated can long <u>endure</u>. We are met on a great battlefield of that war. We have come to dedicate a portion of that field as a final resting-place for those who here gave their lives that that nation might live. It is altogether fitting and proper that we should do this.

But in a larger sense, we cannot dedicate, we cannot <u>consecrate</u>, we cannot hallow

(Continued)

Tweeting to Show Understanding ("Gettysburg Address")

NAME: _____ DATE: _____

DIRECTIONS:

1. Read "The Gettysburg Address" by Abraham Lincoln.
2. Answer the following questions in the space below.
   - Who has perished?
   - Why is this ground being consecrated?
   - What is the proposition set forth for all men?
   - What task should the people be dedicated to?
   - What does Lincoln mean when he says, "We cannot hallow this ground"?
3. Compose a tweet that tells a classmate a main point Lincoln makes in "The Gettysburg Address." Keep your tweet to 140 characters and spaces and try to include one to two new words.

Reprinted from *Vocabulary Is Comprehension* by Laura Robb. Thousand Oaks, CA: Corwin. Reproduction authorized only for the local school site or nonprofit organization that has purchased this book.

(Continued)

this ground. The brave men, living and dead who struggled here have consecrated it far above our poor power to add or detract. The world will little note nor long remember what we say here, but it can never forget what they did here. It is for us the living rather to be dedicated here to the unfinished work which they who fought here have thus far so nobly advanced. It is rather for us to be here dedicated to the great task remaining before us—that from these honored dead we take increased devotion to that cause for which they gave the last full measure of devotion—that we here highly resolve that these dead shall not have died in vain, that this nation under God shall have a new birth of freedom, and that government of the people, by the people, for the people shall not <u>perish</u> from the earth.

Goals: One of the great speeches delivered by a president of the United States, "The Gettysburg Address" is worthy of being studied in history and English. It is a brief 300-word speech that challenges students' ability to listen and to read and comprehend. It's considered one of the most famous speeches in American history because Lincoln turned a speech commemorating those who died in the Battle of Gettysburg into a profound speech that honors the dead and causes listeners to think about the meaning of the Civil War and the union of North and South. This lesson asks students to compose tweets using a vocabulary word that shows depth of understanding. Selected words are *dedicated, proposition, endure, consecrate,* and *perish.* Go to this site for explanations of the tough words in this speech so you can support students: http://www.westmeade.net/Library/GettysburgAddress.html.

Materials: Copies of "The Gettysburg Address" and the reproducible Tweeting to Show Understanding ("The Gettysburg Address") for each student (see **www.corwin .com/vocabularyiscomprehension**), chart paper or whiteboard

Day 1

▶ Give students a copy of "The Gettysburg Address" and read it aloud slowly and dramatically.

▶ Close read the text of "The Gettysburg Address."

▶ Identify the vocabulary in the speech that students might have difficulty with and preteach words without strong context clues: *conceived, proposition, endure, detract.*

▶ Have pairs or small groups discuss what they know about the word, use an online or print dictionary to deepen their knowledge of the word's meaning, and discuss situations where the word works.

▶ Choral read the speech together and encourage students to discuss the speech. Use these questions to stir discussions:

  ○ Can you think of two or three purposes for the speech?

  ○ Why does Lincoln want the dead to not have died in vain?

  ○ Why is "The Gettysburg Address" relevant today?

▶ Work with students to create a chart with the word and its forms, its meaning, and situations it works in.

Day 2

Word and Its Forms	Meaning	Situations
dedicated, dedicate, dedicating, dedication	committed to a cause or belief; devoted	a cause, belief, job, profession, political party
perish, perished, perishing	to die	terminally ill, during war, in an accident
consecrate, consecrated, consecrating, consecrator	to declare sacred	a church, hallowed ground; dedicate your life to God, the church; cemetery to honor soldiers
endure, endured, enduring, endurance	last, lasting, longevity	a marathon, distance swimming, training for any sport, pain, extreme heat or cold, buildings that lasted for centuries
proposition, proposal, propose, proposed, proposing	idea that's set down in words	for marriage, a plan, a statement, business terms, a suggestion, an idea

Words, meaning, and situations.

▶ Have students read the selection several times and discuss the themes in the speech.

Here's what eighth graders said:

"Part of the battlefield will become a cemetery to honor the soldiers who fought and died here; those living must work to keep our country strong and the memory of why these soldiers fought and died; we must keep our government of, by, and for the people."

Day 3

- Organize students into pairs or groups of three to four.

- Remind students that a tweet contains 140 characters and spaces. It's okay if tweets are under 140 characters and spaces, but they can't go over that number.

- Have students compose tweets on a computer or by using the form on the reproducible Tweeting to Show Understanding ("The Gettysburg Address").

- With a computer, students can check the number of characters and spaces in their tweet.

- Post the chart with the words, meanings, and situations (see below).

- Have pairs or groups create a tweet for one word, making sure that there will be a tweet for each word.

> Here's the tweet a pair of eighth graders wrote for _perish_.
>
> "When the driver lost control of the car, it slammed into a tree. Both passengers in front seat _perished._ Two children in back seat survived."

- Ask students to share their tweets with the class.

> Here are two of their tweets:
>
> "The priest used prayer and incense _to consecrate_ land reserved for the cemetery behind the church so members could be buried there."
>
> "Both men _endured_ the physical pain and mental stress of scaling the snow covered trail and ice-glazed rocks that led to the top of mountain."

- Invite students to discuss how word knowledge and tweeting improved their comprehension of "The Gettysburg Address."

> The class agreed that tweeting deepened their understanding of a word and the situations because they had to show their understanding in a limited number of characters and spaces. Knowing the words, students said, "was their ticket to comprehending Lincoln's speech."

Day 4

- Ask students to complete the reproducible Tweeting to Show Understanding ("The Gettysburg Address").

Tips for English Language Learners and Developing Readers

- Have students read a paraphrased version on the website that follows after you read the original: http://www.westmeade.net/Library/GettysburgAddress.html#GettysburgAddress

- Guide this group to select one or two words they can successfully tweet.

▶ Engage students in discussing each word before composing a tweet.

▶ Have students tell you the situation they chose to use the word in.

▶ Circulate to provide scaffolding.

How I Might Follow Up This Lesson

▶ I might have students tweet sentences that illustrate understanding of vocabulary for other complex texts we study. Each time, I would ask students to share their tweets so all students see the range of possibilities.

▶ If students have difficulty composing tweets, I would use the gradual release model. I might work with a few and then move them to independence. I could also have students compose tweets in small groups, then with a partner, and finally on their own.

LESSON 9

Four Words to Respond to Texts

BIG 10 #9 Promote Independent Reading

CCSS 4a, 4b, 4d, 5a, 5b, 5c, 6

Complex Text:

Sojourner Truth's Speech "Ain't I a Woman?"

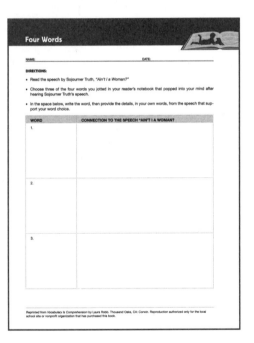

Well, children, where there is so much racket there must be something out of kilter. I think that 'twixt the negroes of the South and the women at the North, all talking about rights, the white men will be in a fix pretty soon. But what's all this here talking about?

That man over there says that women need to be helped into carriages, and lifted over ditches, and to have the best place everywhere. Nobody ever helps me into carriages, or over mud-puddles, or gives me any best place! And ain't I a woman? Look at me! Look at my arm! I have ploughed and planted, and gathered into barns, and no man could head me! And ain't I a woman? I could work as much and eat as much as a man—when I could get it—and bear the lash as well! And ain't I a woman? I have borne thirteen children, and seen most all sold off to slavery, and when I cried out with my mother's grief, none but Jesus heard me! And ain't I a woman?

Then they talk about this thing in the head; what's this they call it? [member of audience whispers, "intellect"] That's it, honey. What's that got to do with women's rights or negroes' rights? If my cup won't hold but a pint, and yours holds a quart, wouldn't you be mean not to let me have my little half measure full?

Then that little man in black there, he says women can't have as much rights as men, 'cause Christ wasn't a woman! Where did your Christ come from? Where did your Christ come from? From God and a woman! Man had nothing to do with Him.

If the first woman God ever made was strong enough to turn the world upside down all alone, these women together ought to be able to turn it back, and get it right side up again! And now they is asking to do it, the men better let them.

Obliged to you for hearing me, and now old Sojourner ain't got nothing more to say.

Note: This is a version of Sojourner Truth's speech as remembered by Frances Gage, president of the 1851 Women's Right Convention where the speech was delivered. For another account of the speech, see https://www.nolo.com/legal-encyclopedia/content/truth-woman-speech.html.

Goals: When students read a speech, poem, or story that is so powerful, so moving, they should have time to process their emotions and thoughts and not immediately plunge into a discussion using text-specific questions or a close reading. In this lesson, they use words that leap into their minds after hearing the speech—words that show reactions to powerful literature. Students will choose three words they generated and link each word to the text by citing specific evidence from the speech.

Materials: Copies of "Ain't I a Woman?" and the reproducible Four Words for each student (see **www.corwin.com/vocabularyiscomprehension**); readers' notebooks

---

Day 1

▸ Provide some background information about Sojourner Truth. Go to this website and have students listen to the audio summary of her life: http://www.biography .com/people/sojourner-truth-9511284.

▸ Read the speech aloud with zeal—as Sojourner herself might have delivered it!

Day 2

▸ Organize students into pairs.

▸ Have partners take turns reading the speech to each other.

▸ Ask students to think of four words that come to mind after hearing this speech and write them in their readers' notebooks.

▸ I share one of my words: *strong.* Next I use details from the speech that support strong. Sojourner Truth was mentally and emotionally strong because she answers the man who says women need help into carriages and stepping over ditches. She tells him and others that no one carried her over a ditch; that she works in the fields as hard as any man; she plows fields, bore thirteen children, and works hard.

▸ Ask students to circle one of their words and write, in their readers' notebooks, specific details from the speech that support their word choice.

▸ Invite students to volunteer and share what they wrote with classmates. This provides students with multiple examples. Here's a sampling from seventh graders:

Word	Connect to the Speech
outspoken	Speaks her beliefs about rights for Negroes in the South and women without fear. Argues her points—starting with the work she can do to pointing out that Eve was a strong woman.
fairness	Wants rights for the negroes of the South and women. Says "intellect" has nothing to do with rights. Says the argument that Christ wasn't a woman doesn't work. Asks, Where did Christ come from? A woman and God.

Seventh-grade students connect words to "Ain't I a Woman?"

▶ Have students complete the reproducible Four Words.

Tips for English Language Learners and Developing Readers

▶ Read the speech out loud two times for ELL students and developing readers.

▶ Ask students to point out words that are unfamiliar. Discuss these with students.

▶ Have students discuss their reactions to the speech and help them find four words, such as *bold, equality, fairness, anger, inner strength, fearless.*

How I Might Follow Up This Lesson

▶ I would definitely use the "four words" strategy with powerful read-alouds and poems and ask students to share their words so they see a range of reactions to the text. I would also ask students to choose one of the words they jotted and in their readers' notebooks link it to the text, citing specific details.

> Smart
> Proving of herself
> Clever
> Strong
>
>
> Strong; She Does Work Men should do
>
> " I have ploughed and planted and gathered into barns, no man Could head me."
>
>
> Clever; When she is asked a question she answers cleverly.
>
> " where did you'r Christ Come from? God and a women, Man had nothing to do with him!"

Rosa quotes from Sojourner Truth's speech to show the connections between the speech and words that were Rosa's initial response to the speech.

Multiple Forms, Multiple Meanings

 Deliver Daily Read-Alouds

CCSS 5a, 5b, 5c, 6

Complex Text:

Excerpt From "The Canterville Ghost" by Oscar Wilde

Multiple Forms, Multiple Meanings

NAME: _____ DATE: _____

DIRECTIONS: Read the excerpt from "The Canterville Ghost" by Oscar Wilde. For each one of the three underlined words do the following:

- Explain the word's meaning based on the way Oscar Wilde uses it.
- Write all the forms of the word; use a dictionary to help.
- Give another meaning of the word and an example.

1. weak

Meaning in text: _____

Other forms of the word: _____

Write another meaning of the word and an example that illustrates the different meaning:

_____

2. shattered

Meaning in text: _____

Other forms of the word: _____

Write another meaning of the word and an example that illustrates the different meaning:

_____

The next day the ghost was very <u>weak</u> and tired. The terrible excitement of the last four weeks was beginning to have its effect. His nerves were completely <u>shattered</u>, and he started at the slightest noise. For five days he kept to his room, and at last made up his mind to give up the point of the blood-stain on the library floor. If the Otis family did not want it, they clearly did not deserve it. They were evidently people on a low, material plane of <u>existence</u>, and quite incapable of appreciating the symbolic value of sensuous phenomena.

Goals: To show students that words have multiple forms and meanings and the context, the way a word is used in a text, determines the word's meaning. Tuning students into multiple meanings of words can enable them to become better users of context clues when reading grade-level complex texts. It also improves their speaking, thinking, and writing vocabulary because they understand the nuanced meanings of the same word in diverse contexts. The selected word is *shattered*.

Materials: Copies of the excerpt and the reproducible Multiple Forms, Multiple Meanings for each student

▶ Review multiple forms of words and multiple meanings. For example, have students discuss and then share with classmates the multiple meanings of *just, justice, justify, justification.*

▶ Provide some brief background about Oscar Wilde and invite students to Google him to learn more about this Irish author born in 1854 and died in 1900. He's best known today for a play, *The Importance of Being Ernest,* and a book, *The Picture of Dorian Gray.* The "Canterville Ghost" is a short story told through the eyes of a most theatrical ghost, Sir Simon.

▶ Give students a copy of the excerpt from "The Canterville Ghost." Read the selection out loud and then ask students to read it silently.

▶ Organize students into pairs.

▶ Have pairs discuss the meaning of *shattered* the way it's used in the third sentence. Fifth-grade students suggested that it means "broken."

▶ Ask partners to think of other meanings for shattered; here's what they say: *burst into pieces as a shattered vase; damage badly as a shattered heart; ruin as a shattered Smart Phone; demolish as a shattered building.*

▶ Invite partners to give other forms of shattered: *shatter, shattering, shatterable.*

▶ Ask students to complete the reproducible Multiple Forms, Multiple Meanings.

Tips for English Language Learners and Developing Readers

▶ Help ELL students and developing readers figure out the different forms of a word.

▶ Show students how you use the words on the reproducible in sentences to show different meanings. Have students discuss the meaning for each sample sentence.

▶ Have students brainstorm different forms of the word. Show them how an online or print dictionary helps with this task.

How I Might Follow Up This Lesson

▶ Since knowing multiple forms and meanings of words is a Common Core standard, I would practice this with instructional texts.

▶ I might also invite students to choose two to four words from their independent reading, noting the page each word was on, and state the multiple forms of the word and its multiple meanings. I would ask students to share their findings with the class or in groups to expand everyone's vocabulary.

◆◆◆ Collaborate and Learn ◆◆◆

Discuss the following four questions/prompts with colleagues or use them to reflect on your own teaching:

1. Bring a lesson you completed to a team or faculty meeting. Discuss what worked and what didn't work. Share written work from a range of students.

2. Why are the CCSS in vocabulary important for teachers of all subjects?

3. Share literacy stories and include teachers from different disciplines who teach vocabulary and discuss how word learning in all subjects can help students.

4. Discuss how vocabulary lessons for the Big 10 teach Tier Two academic vocabulary in the context of reading and why this supports students.

Figurative Language

The rising sun was a lemon drop upon the lip of the shore . . . . I'm so hungry I could eat a horse. . . . I'm bushed . . . You hit the nail on the head. . . .

Figurative language is everywhere in human language. It adds color, spice, mirth, and surprise to our everyday communication. In its broadest sense, it includes figures of speech, idioms, and colloquialisms, to name a few. In conversation, from casual exchanges between buddies to formal State of the Union speeches, figurative language is used to further the connection, to persuade, or to move others. In this chapter, we look at how figurative language is used by writers in the text we read. I'll share lessons that help students feel prepared to wrestle with the meaning of this sophisticated type of usage to the ground. Figurative language is actually quite challenging cognitively, because it asks readers to look at the most common meaning of the words involved— and then quickly sort through alternate possible meanings, word combinations, and connections to interpret the words or phrase.

Whenever I introduce figurative language to students, I ask them to think about this comparison: "A photographer uses a camera to capture a moment and to show how she sees that moment; a writer uses figurative language to show readers how she envisions a moment." In "The Highwayman," a narrative poem by Alfred Noyes, the moment captured by figurative language is a rider on a horse, noticing the light of the moon:

The moon was a ghostly galleon tossed upon cloudy seas

In this instance, the figurative language is in the form of a metaphor, which likens seeing the moon to a pale ship tossed up and down on waves of clouds, which is perfect because the rider, galloping on horseback, would see the moon from this rocking, up-and-down motion vantage point.

It almost goes without saying that complex texts are "complex" depending upon how intricate is the mesh of vocabulary, concepts, and inference. So it stands to reason that figurative language and its heavy load of interpretation plays a big role in text complexity. Therefore, we can help students in a twofold way by explicitly teaching figurative language. First, by exposing them to many examples of it in many textual contexts. Second, by getting them used to the *process* of figuring out this flourished language. Metaphors, for example, can be downright intimidating for our students and we need to give them lots of practice with them. When students know their way around figurative language, they deepen their understanding and, specifically, get better at conjuring visual images while reading. Figurative language moves them from the literal and denotative meanings of words and expressions to the richness of connotative meanings.

Helping Students Not to Be Cowed by Figurative Language

When writers use figurative language in a poem, a story, or an informational text, they create a tight connection between their use of language and readers' interpretation.

Writers know that to craft memorable moments for their reader they have to do better than stating the obvious—the blue bird is blue, the tidal wave was big—and so they use figurative language to help them put their own stamp on a charged moment between two characters, a setting, or other aspect of their text. These fresh combinations of words create visual images and immediacy, and give readers a "you are there" feeling that involves all our senses.

Let's return to the opening of "The Highwayman" (see above). In one line, the reader is on the road, on the galloping horse, believing the moon is a ship tossed on a stormy sea. With a few words, figurative language creates a special effect that captures the attention of the reader and listener. It moves us quickly beyond the denotative or literal meaning to connotations created through unique comparisons (simile and metaphor) or attributing human qualities to a mountain or waves (personification).

What's remarkable about figurative language is that the metaphor or simile can trigger a personal memory and enrich the reading and listening even more. For example, whenever someone describes a certain scent with the figurative expression, "like ambrosia cooking on Mount Olympus," I am transported back into Grandma Annie's kitchen, smelling her pot roast simmering in the heavy iron pot.

As students apply their knowledge of figurative language to the texts they read independently, it improves their writing as well as their reading comprehension. They develop a sense of how these tools can support *their* writing, and they naturally integrate metaphor, simile, connotative meanings, and the like into their own texts.

Guidelines for Reading Poetry

The lessons in this chapter use poetry because poets so often use figurative language to communicate with readers. Here are some guidelines for reading poems that help students learn to savor the poet's language phrase by phrase and line by line.

▶ Read the poem aloud to the class and model fluent, expressive reading.

▶ Organize students into partners and give each student a copy of the poem. With partnerships, there's a solid chance that both students talk. In a group, it's easy for a student not to respond and difficult for the teacher to monitor who's contributing when four to five groups work at the same time. Once pairs discuss, you can invite them to join another pair and share what they discussed.

Additional Poems Online
See www.corwin.com/ vocabularyiscomprehension for extra poems to use for Lessons 1 through 6 for reteaching or providing students with extra practice. And use poems you love and ones that connect to your curriculum. At the website, you'll also find a set of reproducible forms to use with ELLs and developing readers to support their learning.

▶ Ask partners to take turns reading the poem aloud several times. Students can take turns reading the entire poem or different stanzas. Explain that all you want them to do at this point is to listen to the language, enjoying the rhythms and images the poem kindles.

▶ Have students pair-share their reactions and responses to the poem. Responses can include telling about emotional feelings, discussing a line or stanza that spoke to them, and asking questions the poem raised.

▶ Ask students to reread the poem silently and to summarize in their notebooks their discussions and any new ideas that surfaced.

Two More Lessons and More About Figurative Language
For a lesson on personification see pages 26-30, and for a lesson on denotative and connotative meanings of words see pages 44-48 in Chapter 2.
Also see the handout More About Figurative Language at **www.corwin.com/ vocabularyiscomprehension**

Alliteration

Complex Text:

First Stanza From "The Raven" by Edgar Allan Poe

> Once upon a midnight dreary, while I pondered
>   weak and weary,   1
> Over many a quaint and curious volume of
>   forgotten lore,   2
> While I nodded, nearly napping, suddenly there
>   came a tapping,   3
> As of someone gently rapping, rapping at my
>   chamber door.   4
> "Tis some visitor," I muttered, "tapping at my
>   chamber door—   5
> Only this and nothing more."   6

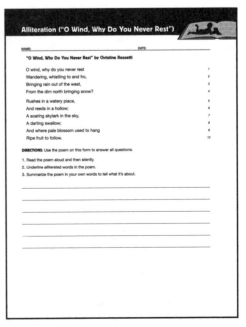

Alliteration ("Three Things to Remember")

NAME: _____ DATE: _____

"Three Things to Remember" by William Blake

A Robin Redbreast in a cage,	1
Puts all Heaven in a rage.	2
A skylark wounded on the wing	3
Doth make a cherub cease to sing.	4
He who shall hurt the little wren	5
Shall never be beloved by men.	6

DIRECTIONS: Use the poem on this form to answer all questions.

1. Read the poem aloud in a soft voice and then silently.

2. Underline alliterated words in the poem.

3. Explain the theme or main point of this poem.

_____
_____
_____
_____

4. How does alliteration emphasize the poem's meaning?

_____
_____
_____
_____

5. How is the alliteration in lines 1 and 2 connected to alliteration in lines 3 and 4?

_____
_____
_____
_____

Reprinted from *Vocabulary is Comprehension* by Laura Robb. Thousand Oaks, CA: Corwin. Reproduction authorized only for the local
school site or nonprofit organization that has purchased this book.

Alliteration ("O Wind, Why Do You Never Rest")

NAME: _____ DATE: _____

"O Wind, Why Do You Never Rest" by Christina Rossetti

O wind, why do you never rest	1
Wandering, whistling to and fro,	2
Bringing rain out of the west,	3
From the dim north bringing snow?	4
Rushes in a watery place,	5
And reeds in a hollow,	6
A soaring skylark in the sky,	7
A darting swallow;	8
And where pale blossom used to hang	9
Ripe fruit to follow.	10

DIRECTIONS: Use the poem on this form to answer all questions.

1. Read the poem aloud and then silently.

2. Underline alliterated words in the poem.

3. Summarize the poem in your own words to tell what it's about.

_____
_____
_____
_____
_____
_____

Goals: We want students to see how writers use alliteration to call attention to specific words to create a mood, raise an emotion, or highlight a theme. We want them to understand that alliteration is the repetition of the same sounds at the beginning of words or in stressed syllables. For example, in his poem "The Lake Isle of Innisfree" William Butler Yeats repeats the initial "l" sound in *lake, lapping,* and *low.* In doing so, the poet helps us imagine the low and gentle sounds of water repeatedly touching the shore.

Materials: Copies of the first stanza of "The Raven," the reproducible "Three Things" for proficient and advanced readers, and the reproducible "O Wind" for ELLs and developing readers (see **www.corwin.com/vocabularyiscomprehension**), chart paper or whiteboard

---

Day 1

▶ Give students a copy of the first stanza of "The Raven."

▶ Read the selection out loud and ask students to share words or phrases that they need to have clarified.

> *Eighth graders request more information for* pondered *and* volume of forgotten lore. *Students worked with partners to see if context could help them figure out these words. Here's what a pair noted:*
>
> *"Well, Poe's pondering a volume of forgotten lore. Here pondering means reading and thinking about a volume or a book. Forgotten lore might mean stories that are old and have been forgotten."*

▶ Help students understand all the words they offer. If context doesn't help, then use an online dictionary.

▶ Ask partners to take turns reading the stanza to each another.

After reading the first stanza of "The Raven" aloud, ask students to partner up and take turns reading the stanza to each other.

Day 2

▶ Have students turn to the same partner they worked with on Day 1 and do a 2-minute share on everything they know about alliteration.

▶ Have partners pool their ideas with a pair close to them and choose a spokesperson to share with the entire class.

▶ Ask each spokesperson to share the group's ideas while you record the thinking on chart paper or a whiteboard.

▶ Read aloud the Poe stanza. Point out the alliteration in the poem's first line: *weak* and *weary* and explain how these words show the poet is tired of thinking. It takes readers back to midnight and how long the poet has been pondering.

{ *Eighth graders noted that I thought about the alliterated words' meanings and connected this to what the poet was doing.*

▶ Ask pairs to find other examples of alliteration in the stanza and explain the connotations and connections.

{ *Here's what a pair said about* nodded, nearly napping:

"It shows that the poet was sleepy and maybe bored with the reading. That takes us back to weary— tired of doing this. We can feel the poet is drowsy, nodding like he's falling asleep. This sleepy mood changes with the word tapping.*"*

▶ Ask students to explain alliteration and how it functions, encouraging them to use the text to support their ideas. Encourage them to bring examples from their independent reading to share.

Day 3

▶ Have students complete the reproducible "Three Things to Remember" or "O Wind".

Tips for English Language Learners and Developing Readers

▶ Confer one-to-one or in a small group to determine that these students understand alliteration.

▶ Use one of the poems online at **www.corwin.com/vocabularyiscompre hension** to offer these students extra practice.

▶ Help those who require it complete the reproducible.

How I Might Follow Up This Lesson

▶ I might have the entire class or a group practice pinpointing alliteration and discussing how it improves their comprehension of the poem.

▶ I might also work with students to extend their thinking about the function of alliteration, showing how alliteration can create a mood, return them to other words and ideas, and generate connotations.

Alliteration points to the theme. While discussing alliteration with Emma, Ryan said that alliteration is the poet's way of highlighting big ideas.

Alliteration ("Three Things to Remember")

NAME: Emma C   DATE:

"Three Things to Remember" by William Blake

A Robin Redbreast in a cage,   1
Puts all Heaven in a rage.   2

A skylark wounded on the wing   3
Doth make a cherub cease to sing.   4

He who shall hurt the little wren   5
Shall never be beloved by men.   6

DIRECTIONS: Use the poem on this form to answer all questions.

1. Read the poem aloud in a soft voice and then silently.

2. Underline alliterated words in the poem.

3. Explain the theme or main point of this poem.

Let wild birds be fierce and free
Keep nature safe and free
Consequence comes from wrongdoing think before you do
Treat people how you want to be treated

4. How does alliteration emphasize the poem's meaning?

Shows main point

5. How is the alliteration in lines 1 and 2 connected to alliteration in lines 3 and 4?

They are both about birds being badly treated
and the consequence that comes for that.

Metaphor

Complex Text:

"She Sweeps With Many Colored Brooms" by Emily Dickinson

She sweeps with many-colored brooms,	1
And leaves the shreds behind;	2
Oh, housewife in the evening west,	3
Come back, and dust the pond!	4
You dropped a purple ravelling in,	5
You dropped an amber thread;	6
And now you've littered all the East	7
With duds of emerald!	8
And still she plies her spotted brooms,	9
And still the aprons fly,	10
Till brooms fade softly into stars—	11
And then I come away.	12

Metaphor ("The Highwayman")

NAME: _____ DATE: _____

First Stanza of "The Highwayman" by Alfred Noyes

The wind was a torrent of darkness among the gusty trees,	1
The moon was a ghostly galleon tossed upon cloudy seas,	2
The road was a ribbon of moonlight over the purple moor,	3
And the highwayman came riding—	4
Riding—riding—	5
The highwayman came riding, up to the old inn-door.	6

DIRECTIONS: Read the poem twice and then answer the questions below.

1. Define metaphor.

_____

_____

2. Identify two metaphors in the poem and explain how the metaphor relates to the setting.

_____

_____

_____

3. Explain the mood the metaphors create and cite specific words and phrases that help develop this mood.

_____

_____

_____

_____

Reprinted from *Vocabulary Is Comprehension* by Laura Robb. Thousand Oaks, CA: Corwin. Reproduction authorized only for the local school site or nonprofit organization that has purchased this book.

Metaphor ("Forecast")

NAME: _____ DATE: _____

"Forecast" by Anina Robb

We waited all day for the snowfall.	1
But we were snowed.	2
This Winter was a cheat, a windbag	3
full of icy promises and shutter-rattling oaths.	4
After all, Winter is supposed to be	5
a promise for every school child:	6
lazy mornings, sledding, hot chocolate,	7
and boredom all wrapped up in a prediction.	8

DIRECTIONS: Read the poem aloud and then silently and answer the questions below.

1. Define metaphor.

_____

_____

_____

_____

2. Why does the poet call winter a cheat and a windbag?

_____

_____

_____

_____

_____

Goals: With this lesson, our aim is for students to understand extended metaphor and appreciate how Dickinson's image of the housewife helps them experience the change from day to dusk to evening. Students should learn that metaphor is an abstract comparison of two unlike things; metaphors equate two things by using the verbs *is* and *are*. Often, poets used an extended metaphor, one that threads through all the poem's lines or stanzas.

Materials: Copies of Dickinson's poem, the reproducible "The Highwayman" for proficient and advanced readers, and the reproducible "Forecast" for ELLs and developing readers (see **www.corwin.com/vocabularyiscomprehension**)

Day 1

▶ Organize students into pairs.

▶ Read the poem out loud.

▶ Invite pairs to take turns and read the poem to one another to see if they can find the metaphor.

▶ Use an online dictionary to help students understand words that don't have strong context clues: *ravelling, duds*—and ask students to discuss each word's meaning in relation to the poem.

▶ Ask the same pairs to annotate their copy of the poem to see if they can figure out Dickinson's extended metaphor.

▶ In this poem, Emily Dickinson uses an extended metaphor of the housewife.

Two pairs of sixth graders, through annotating the poem, figure out the metaphor. Here's what they observed: "Apron was a huge clue and broom too," they said. "And then it was easy to see she [housewife] was cleaning day away." }

Day 2

▶ Invite the same pairs to identify all the words that link to the metaphor of housewife.

Sixth graders offered these: sweeps, dust, littered, plies, fly. }

▶ Ask students to think on their own and explain how the metaphor of the housewife and the verbs they identified support their understanding.

Here's what a student said:

"A traditional housewife cleans her house. In this poem, the housewife cleans away day and adds items that forecast evening is coming. She wears an apron and carries a broom just like a housewife. By using the housewife metaphor she [Dickinson] brings energy and motion to the poem. After dusting the pond, the housewife's aprons fly, putting on the final touches that change dusk into night. The housewife leads us through the changes, and the metaphor made us remember sunsets we watched." }

Day 3

▶ Have students complete the reproducible "The Highwayman" or "Forecast."

Tips for English Language Learners and Developing Readers

▶ If the Emily Dickinson poem is too challenging, find a poem that students can read easily with a metaphor that's accessible to them. Read the poem to them; ask pairs to read it to each other. Discuss the metaphor and the images it paints, the memories it triggers, and how these support understanding.

▶ Help those who require it complete the reproducible "Forecast."

How I Might Follow Up This Lesson

▶ If all or a group of students would benefit from extra practice, I would use a poem from the website (**www.corwin.com/vocabularyiscomprehension**) and repeat the lesson.

▶ I might challenge students to return to a first draft of a poem, story, or informational piece they've written and find a place where they could add a metaphor.

Lavie, a seventh grader, uses the metaphors to determine the mood.

Metaphor ("The Highwayman")

NAME: _____ DATE: _____

First Stanza of "The Highwayman" by Alfred Noyes

The wind was a torrent of darkness among the gusty trees,	1
The moon was a ghostly galleon tossed upon cloudy seas,	2
The road was a ribbon of moonlight over the purple moor,	3
And the highwayman came riding—	4
Riding—riding—	5
The highwayman came riding, up to the old inn-door.	6

DIRECTIONS: Read the poem twice and then answer the questions below.

1. Define metaphor.

Comparison between 2 different things without using like or as. Makes two things equal.

2. Identify two metaphors in the poem and explain how the metaphor relates to the setting.

*The wind was a torrent among the gusty trees-very windy weather. *The moon was a ghostly galleon - The man is bouncing so the moon goes up and down.

3. Explain the mood the metaphors create and cite specific words and phrases that help develop this mood.

Mood: Eerie or haunting
"Torrent of darkness"
"Purple moor"
"Ghostly galleon"

Onomatopoeia

Complex Text:

Excerpt From "The Village Blacksmith" by Henry Wadsworth Longfellow

Week in, week out, from morn till night,	1
You can hear his bellows <u>blow</u>;	2
You can hear him <u>swing</u> his heavy sledge,	3
With measured <u>beat</u> and slow,	4
Like a sexton <u>ringing</u> the village <u>bell</u>,	5
When the evening sun is low.	6
And children coming home from school	7
Look in at the open door;	8
They love to see the flaming forge,	9
And hear the bellows <u>roar</u>,	10
And catch the burning sparks that fly	11
Like chaff from a <u>threshing-floor</u>.	12

Onomatopoeia ("A Train Went Through a Burial Ground")

NAME: _____ DATE: _____

"A Train Went Through a Burial Ground" by Emily Dickinson

A train went through a burial gate,	1
A bird broke forth and sang,	2
And trilled, and quivered, and shook his throat	3
Till all the churchyard rang;	4
And then adjusted his little notes,	5
And bowed and sang again.	6
Doubtless, he thought it meet of him	7
To say good-by to men.	8

DIRECTIONS: Read the poem twice and discuss its meaning with a partner.

1. Define onomatopoeia.

_____
_____
_____
_____

2. Underline all the onomatopoeic words in the poem.

_____
_____
_____

3. Discuss the changes in the sound words and how these connect to the poem's main idea.

_____
_____
_____
_____
_____

Reprinted from *Vocabulary Is Comprehension* by Laura Robb. Thousand Oaks, CA: Corwin. Reproduction authorized only for the local school site or nonprofit organization that has purchased this book.

Onomatopoeia ("Bedtime")

NAME: _____ DATE: _____

"Bedtime" by Anina Robb

My Nanna told me the	1
rump-rump rattle	2
of the number 2 train	3
under my window	4
was just the sand man	5
splattering my dreams	6
for the night	7
along the line.	8
So now when I hear the	9
9 o'clock whistle	10
I know it's nothing	11
to worry about, it's just	12
my wishes—and I blow:	13
Shush, shush.	14

DIRECTIONS: Read the poem aloud and then silently and answer the questions below.

1. Define onomatopoeia.

_____
_____
_____
_____

2. Underline all the onomatopoeic words in the poem.

Goals: We want students to understand that onomatopoeic words imitate the sounds associated with *actions* the words refer to or with *objects*. For example, in the third stanza of this Longfellow poem, the poet includes onomatopoeic words so readers hear and picture the village blacksmith working diligently in his shop. The fourth stanza is from the children's perspective and reinforces the sounds that result from the blacksmith's work. Onomatopoeia can point to emotions, a mood, a theme, or in narrative poems, these words help us learn about characters.

Materials: Copies of third and fourth stanzas of "The Village Blacksmith," the reproducible "A Train Went Through a Burial Ground" for proficient and advanced readers, and the reproducible "Bedtime" for ELLs and developing readers (also see **www.corwin.com/vocabularyiscomprehension** for the reproducibles and the entire poem of "The Village Blacksmith")

Day 1

▶ Organize students into pairs.

▶ Read both stanzas out loud.

▶ Have partners read the stanzas to one another, listening for the words that create sounds.

▶ Invite individual students to share unfamiliar words.

Seventh graders offer forge, chaff, threshing-floor.

▶ Use an online dictionary for these words and invite pairs to discuss the meaning of each word as it's used in the poem.

One pair points out that in the poem forge *means a furnace and* <u>not</u> *imitating a signature or creating fake money or documents.*

Another pair says that chaff *is the husks of corn or wheat that comes from threshing or beating the grain to separate seeds. It can also mean to thrash about as in your sleep. The simile "Like chaff from a threshing-floor" lets you see how the sparks fly in the air as the children try to catch them.*

Day 2

▶ Ask different pairs to reread the stanzas to one another.

▶ Have partners identify the onomatopoeic words and explain the sounds they hear.

"It's like the poem has its own sound effects," one student said.

Day 3

▶ Ask students to complete the reproducible "A Train Went Through a Burial Ground" or the reproducible "Bedtime."

Jennifer, a fifth-grade ELL student, shows her understanding of onomatopoeia in her answers for 1 to 5.

Onomatopoeia ("Bedtime")

NAME: _Jennifer Pineda_   DATE: _____

"Bedtime" by Anina Robb

My Nanna told me the	1
rump-rump rattle	2
of the number 2 train	3
under my window	4
was just the sand man	5
splattering my dreams	6
for the night	7
along the line.	8
So now when I hear the	9
9 o'clock whistle	10
I know it's nothing	11
to worry about, it's just	12
my wishes—and I blow:	13
Shush, shush.	14

DIRECTIONS: Read the poem aloud and then silently and answer the questions below.

1. Define onomatopoeia.

Ex: "shush-shush, thump, crash, whoosh"
sounds

_____

_____

_____

2. Underline all the onomatopoeic words in the poem.

3. Which words help you hear the train?

rump—rump rattle, whistle,

blow

4. Why does the poet write "and I blow?"

The girl is trying to be like the

train.

5. Who speaks the "Shush, Shush?" Explain why.

Nanna, because she says the

girl has to go to bed

Tips for English Language Learners and Developing Readers

▶ Give students situations that are ripe for onomatopoeic words—a storm, grilling meat, dancing, chopping wood, running, slicing bread, a busy city street, and so. Ask them to close their eyes and imagine the situation, the actions involved. What sounds come to mind? How might we come up with words to represent those sounds?

▶ Because visualizing is an indication of understanding, have students draw what they visualize and hear.

▶ Help those who require it complete the reproducible "Bedtime."

How I Might Follow Up This Lesson

▶ To reinforce that writers of narrative and informational texts also use onomatopoeia, I would ask students to find examples from their instruction and/or independent reading to share with classmates.

▶ I might ask students to find a place in one of their drafts where they could effectively use onomatopoeic words.

Repetition

Complex Text:

"Lord Randal" by Author Unknown, a Traditional Anglo-Scottish Ballad

"O where have you been, Lord Randal, my son? 1
And where have you been, my handsome
    young man?" 2
"I've been at the greenwood; mother, make my
    bed soon, 3
For I'm wearied with hunting, and fain
    would lie down." 4

"And who met you there, Lord Randal, my son? 5
And who met you there, my handsome young man?" 6
"O I met with my true-love; mother, make
    my bed soon, 7
For I'm wearied with hunting, and fain would lie down." 8

"And what did she give you, Lord Randal, my son? 9
And what did she give you, my handsome
    young man?" 10
"Eels fried in a pan; mother, make my bed soon, 11
For I'm wearied with hunting, and fain
    would lie down." 12

"And who got your scraps, Lord Randal, my son? 13
And who got your scraps, my handsome young man?" 14

(Continued)

77

(Continued)

"My hawks and my hounds; mother, make my bed soon,   15
For I'm wearied with hunting, and fain
     would lie down."   16

"And what became of them, Lord Randal, my son?   17
And what became of them, my handsome young man?"   18
"They stretched their legs out and died; mother,
     make my bed soon,   19
For I'm wearied with hunting, and fain would
     lie down."   20

"O I fear you are poisoned, Lord Randal, my son!   21
I fear you are poisoned, my handsome young man!"   22
"O yes, I am poisoned; mother, make my bed soon,   23
For I'm sick at the heart, and I fain would lie down." 24

"What d'ye leave to your mother,
     Lord Randal, my son?   25
What d'ye leave to your mother,
     my handsome young man?"   26
"Four and twenty milk cows; mother,
     make my bed soon,   27
For I'm sick at heart, and I fain would lie down."   28

"What d'ye leave to your sister, Lord Randal, my son? 29
What d'ye leave to your sister, my handsome
     young man?"   30
"My gold and my silver; mother, make my bed soon,   31
For I'm sick at heart, and I fain would lie down."   32

"What d'ye leave to your brother, Lord Randal, my son?   33
What d'ye leave to your brother, my handsome
          young man?"   34
"My houses and my lands; mother, make my bed soon,   35
For I'm sick at heart, and I fain would lie down."   36

"What d'ye leave to your true-love, Lord Randal
          my son?   37
What d'ye leave to your true-love, my handsome
          young man?"   38
"I leave her hell and fire; mother, make my bed soon,   39
For I'm sick at heart, and I fain would lie down."   40

Repetition ("It's All I Have to Bring Today")

NAME: _____   DATE: _____

"It's All I Have to Bring Today" by Emily Dickinson

It's all I have to bring today—   1
This, and my heart beside—   2
This, and my heart, and all the fields—   3
And all the meadows wide—   4
Be sure you count—should I forget   5
Some one the sum could tell—   6
This, and my heart, and all the Bees   7
Which in the Clover dwell.   8

DIRECTIONS: Read the poem twice.

1. Use poem details to explain how this is a poem about the rebirth of spring.

_____
_____
_____
_____

2. What does the repeated phrase "and my heart" let you know about the poet's feelings?

_____
_____
_____
_____

Repetition ("If I Can Stop One Heart From Breaking")

NAME: _____   DATE: _____

"If I Can Stop One Heart From Breaking" by Emily Dickinson

If I can stop one heart from breaking,   1
I shall not live in vain;   2
If I can ease one life the aching,   3
Or cool one pain,   4
Or help one fainting robin   5
Unto his nest again,   6
I shall not live in vain.   7

DIRECTIONS: Read the poem aloud and then silently. Use details in the poem to answer the questions.

1. Underline the repeated lines and phrases.
2. Explain the meaning of vain as used in the poem. Use an online or print dictionary to help.

_____
_____
_____
_____

3. What does Dickinson see as a great purpose of her life?

_____
_____
_____

Goals: This is one of the oldest ballads in the English language. Some historians believe that Lord Randal might be Randolph, sixth Earl of Chester who was poisoned by his wife and died in 1232. Clearly, it's a complex text for students, but with rereading and discussion, students come to understand and enjoy it. Our aim in general is to show students that they have the tools to tame intimidating texts and that it's worth the effort. In particular, we want students to see techniques such as the repeating of a word within a sentence, a poetical line within a stanza, or a refrain repeated at the end of each stanza. We want them to notice that repetitions can occur throughout a poem. We want them to appreciate that repeated lines, phrases, or words can foreshadow an event, comment on an event or moment, emphasize a point, or produce specific sounds or emotions.

In "Lord Randal," the repeated line foreshadows the impending death of Lord Randal at the hands of his true love. Readers learn about Lord Randal's impending death in the sixth stanza when Randal's mother says that she fears her son has been poisoned.

Materials: Copy of "Lord Randal," the reproducible "It's All I Have to Bring Today" for proficient and advanced readers and the reproducible "If I Can Stop One Heart From Breaking" for ELLs and developing readers (see **www.corwin.com/ vocabularyiscomprehension**)

Day 1

▸ Read the ballad out loud.

▸ Organize students into groups of four and have them take turns reading the stanzas to each other.

▸ Ask groups to discuss the narrative elements in this ballad.

> *A group of fifth graders points out that it tells a story and has characters—Lord Randal, his mother, and the sweetheart. It also has dialogue. Another pair says that the plot moves on with the mom asking questions and her son answering them.*

Day 2

▸ Have students identify the repeated line and discuss its function in the ballad.

> *All students agreed that the repetition foreshadowed Lord Randal's death.*
>
> *One pair explained that the repeated line showed Lord Randal's feelings—he's sick to the heart because his girlfriend poisoned him and he will die. They said that he was a good son 'cause he answered all the questions when all he wanted to do was lie down and be comfortable.*

▸ Have students complete the reproducible "It's All I Have to Bring Today" or "If I Can Stop One Heart From Breaking."

Tips for English Language Learners and Developing Readers

▸ Meet with students and have them retell the story line to make sure they understand the plot.

▸ Ask them to draw the plot on a storyboard and write a caption for each illustration and use their storyboard to retell the plot.

▸ Help those who require it complete the reproducible "If I Can Stop One Heart From Breaking."

How I Might Follow Up This Lesson

▶ To help students see that repetition in poetry and narratives can improve comprehension of character, theme, and plot, I would have them read another traditional ballad and a literary ballad where the author is known (see the website **www.corwin.com/vocabularyiscomprehension** for other traditional ballads).

▶ I might also have students revisit poems they wrote to see if adding repetition could enhance their piece.

Olivia sees how moved Dickinson is by nature and the coming of spring.

Repetition ("It's All I Have to Bring Today")

NAME: Olivia Adams   **DATE:**

"It's All I Have to Bring Today" by Emily Dickenson

It's all I have to bring today—	1
This, and my heart beside—	2
This, and my heart, and all the fields—	3
And all the meadows wide—	4
Be sure you count—should I forget	5
Some one the sum could tell—	6
This, and my heart, and all the Bees	7
Which in the Clover dwell.	8

DIRECTIONS: Read the poem twice.

1. Use poem details to explain how this is a poem about the rebirth of spring.

This poem is about the rebirth of spring because Emily Dickinson uses the words bees, clover, meadows, and fields.

2. What does the repeated phrase "and my heart" let you know about the poet's feelings?

The phrase "and my heart" tells you about the poets feelings by showing that she will always have her heart to give.

3. Why does the poet end with bees in the clover?

The poet ends the poem with bees in the clover because it shows that spring is here, which the rest of the poem was leading up to.

4. Explain the connection between the first line of the poem and the phrase "and my heart."

The connection between the first line of the poem and the phrase "and my heart" shows that the poet feels that her heart is all she has to give.

Simile

Complex Text:

"There Is No Frigate Like a Book" by Emily Dickinson

There is no Frigate like a Book	1
To take us Lands away,	2
Nor any Coursers like a Page	3
Of prancing Poetry.	4
This Traverse may the poorest take	5
Without oppress of Toll—	6
How frugal is the Chariot	7
That bears the Human soul.	8

Simile ("Flint")

NAME: _____ DATE: _____

"Flint" by Christina Rossetti

An emerald is as green as grass,	1
A ruby red as blood;	2
A sapphire shines as blue as heaven;	3
A flint lies in the mud.	4
A diamond is a brilliant stone,	5
To catch a world's desire;	6
An opal holds a fiery spark;	7
But a flint holds fire.	8

DIRECTIONS: Read the poem twice and answer the questions using details from the poem.

1. What is flint? If you're unsure, look it up in an online dictionary.

_____

_____

_____

_____

2. Why does the poet call the poem "Flint?"

_____

_____

_____

_____

Simile ("Frost")

NAME: _____ DATE: _____

"Frost" by Anina Robb

I wanted to say	1
The snow is like cotton balls	2
but is so cold that the snow	3
is as crunchy as popcorn beneath my boots.	4
With every step it's a crackle	5
and a pop like the kindling	6
in the fire that I wish	7
I were beside.	8

DIRECTIONS: Read the poem aloud and then silently. Answer the questions using details from the poem.

1. What does the poet compare snow to in the first stanza?

_____

_____

2. How does the simile in the second stanza help you hear steps in the snow?

_____

_____

_____

3. Can you find two onomatopoeic words and explain why these help you enjoy the poem?

_____

_____

_____

_____

Goals: With this lesson, we want students to understand simile and recognize how this type of comparison builds strong visual images. Students should know that simile is a figure of speech that compares two unlike things that have something in common. A simile uses *like* or *as* to make the comparison. Over time, we want students to discover that fully understanding an author's similes helps them grasp theme and main idea.

In this two-stanza poem, Dickinson compares books to frigates (boats) and coursers (horses) to show how books can take us to the past, into the future, and introduce us to people and places around the world. Since the similes and images evoke travel and movement—*sailing, prancing, traverse, chariot*—they convey the motion, energy, pleasure, and new experiences that books offer.

Materials: Copies of the Emily Dickinson poem, the reproducible "Flint" for proficient and advanced readers and the reproducible "Frost" for ELL and developing readers (see **www.corwin.com/vocabularyiscomprehension**)

Day 1

- Read the poem out loud.
- Organize students into pairs and ask them to take turns reading the poem out loud.
- Ask individuals to underline words on the poem—words whose meaning they're unsure of and share these with the class.

Seventh graders offer frigate, coursers, traverse, frugal.

- Use an online dictionary to help students determine the meanings of these words so they match the poet's context.

Day 2

- Invite the same pairs to discuss the similes in the first stanza.

Here's what students said:

"She [Dickinson] compares a frigate to a book. A frigate is a boat that can travel to different places, but she says a book is better and can take you to more and better places.

"The second simile compares a book of poetry to riding a horse and reading poetry is even better than riding a horse."

- Ask students to find the words that relate to travel and discuss these.

Students offer frigate, coursers, prancing, lands away, traverse, toll. *They agree that all the words make you feel like you're moving to other places—to lands away. And you can get a book free at a library and not pay a fare or toll.*

Day 3

- Have students complete the reproducible "Flint" or "Frost."

Olivia, a seventh grader, uses simile to see the beauty in "Flint."

Simile ("Flint")

NAME: *Olivia Adams*   DATE:

"Flint" by Christina Rossetti

An emerald is as green as grass,	1
A ruby red as blood;	2
A sapphire shines as blue as heaven;	3
A flint lies in the mud.	4
A diamond is a brilliant stone,	5
To catch a world's desire;	6
An opal holds a fiery spark;	7
But a flint holds fire.	8

DIRECTIONS: Read the poem twice and answer the questions using details from the poem.

1. What is flint? If you're unsure, look it up in an online dictionary.

Flint is a type of rock that you can start a fire with.

2. Why does the poet call the poem "Flint?"

The poem is called flint because that is the main focus of the poem.

3. Explain the mood in lines 1 to 3 and how the similes create this mood.

The mood in lines 1 to 3 is somewhat happy because it is talking about the beautiful stones.

4. Why does the mood change in line 4?

The mood changes in line 4 because in that line it switches from the nice stones to the flint in the mud and makes it seem useless.

5. Explain the meaning of "But a flint holds fire." Include connotations in your explanation.

"But a flint holds fire." means that even though the other stones may be beautiful the flint is the most useful because it can cook food.

Tips for English Language Learners and Developing Readers

▶ To deepen students' knowledge of simile, help them compose original similes for items they suggest from daily life, such as hair, bus, fingers, eyes, and so on.

▶ Find other poems with simile and discuss these with students (see **www.corwin.com/vocabularyiscomprehension**).

▶ Help those who require it complete the reproducible "Frost."

How I Might Follow Up This Lesson

▶ I might have a lesson on meter and show students the connection between "prancing poetry" and metric foot.

▶ To help students see the diversity of simile in literature, I would ask them to bring in examples from song lyrics, their independent reading, and overheard conversations.

Tania, a fifth grader whose second language is English, understands the poem's sounds through simile.

Symbols and Symbolism

Complex Text:

"The Road Not Taken" by Robert Frost

Two roads diverged in a yellow wood	1
And sorry I could not travel both	2
And be one traveler, long I stood	3
And looked down one as far as I could	4
To where it bent in the undergrowth;	5
Then took the other, as just as fair	6
And having perhaps the better claim,	7
Because it was grassy and wanted wear;	8
Though as for that, the passing there	9
Had worn them really about the same,	10
And both that morning equally lay	11
In leaves no step had trodden black.	12
Oh, I kept the first for another day!	13
Yet knowing how way leads on to way,	14
I doubted if I should ever come back.	15
I shall be telling this with a sigh	16
Somewhere ages and ages hence:	17
Two roads diverged in a wood and I—	18
I took the one less traveled by,	19
And that has made all the difference.	20

**Symbols and Symbolism
("Land of Counterpane")**

NAME: _____ DATE: _____

"Land of Counterpane" by Robert Louis Stevenson

When I was sick and lay a-bed,   1
I had two pillows at my head,   2
And all my toys beside me lay,   3
To keep me happy all the day.   4

And sometimes for an hour or so   5
I watched my leaden soldiers go,   6
With different uniforms and drills,   7
Among the bed-clothes, through the hills;   8

And sometimes sent my ships in fleets   9
All up and down among the sheets;   10
Or brought my trees and houses out,   11
And planted cities all about.   12

I was the giant great and still   13
That sits upon the pillow-hill,   14
And sees before him, dale and plain,   15
The pleasant land of counterpane.   16

DIRECTIONS: Read the poem twice and answer the questions using details from the poem.

1. What is a counterpane? What does it symbolize in this poem?

_____

_____

_____

_____

Symbols and Symbolism ("Fog")

NAME: _____ DATE: _____

"Fog" by Carl Sandburg

The fog comes   1
on little cat feet.   2
It sits looking   3
over harbor and city   4
on silent haunches   5
and then moves on.   6

DIRECTIONS: Read the poem aloud and then silently. Answer the questions using details from the poem.

1. How does the author personify fog? Evaluate this choice.

_____

_____

_____

_____

_____

2. How does personifying the fog help you visualize fog?

_____

_____

_____

_____

_____

Goals:
With this lesson, we want students to understand the role of symbols. Symbolism is the use of one object to represent something else. Symbolism offers writers opportunities to express double or even multiple levels of meaning. Everyday examples are white symbolizes purity, our flag symbolizes America and patriotism, a rose symbolizes love.

In Frost's poem, the two roads symbolize the choices we make during our lives as well as our individual paths that symbolize the life we've led.

Materials:
Copies of the poem "The Road Not Taken," the reproducible "The Land of Counterpane" for proficient and advanced readers and the reproducible "Fog" for ELL and developing readers (see **www.corwin.com/ vocabularyiscomprehension**)

Day 1

▸ Read the poem out loud.

▸ Organize students into groups of four and have each member read a stanza of the poem out loud to one another.

▸ Have each member from the groups of four summarize one stanza of the poem in order to understand that these roads differed greatly only in Frost's memory.

{ *Here's a sixth grader's summary of stanza 2: "In the second stanza Frost says that the roads were equally worn, making you think that they were the same."*

Another pair jumped in and pointed out that in the last stanza, he says he took the road less traveled by.

"Why this contradiction?" I ask.

"Maybe," a student suggested, "he's trying to convince himself that he took the better road—the one less traveled."

"Any other interpretations?" I ask.

"Yeah," a pair blurt out. "We think that memory changes things. So he remembers it in a different way. Maybe so he won't have regrets because he can't go back."

▶ Encourage such discussions as they offer diverse interpretations and enrich the experience for all students.

▶ Invite groups to collaborate to identify the symbols in this poem and explain their meaning using details from the poem.

Day 2

Students identified two symbols for the road:

"Because there were two roads that diverged, the roads symbolize the choices all of us have to make in life. Sometimes we can't do it all—travel both roads, but can only follow one. Going back and redoing choices is pretty impossible and that's what he [Frost] is saying.

"The road also symbolizes our path of life—the life we live. The poem shows this with the choice, and then the poet looks into the future and how he might feel."

▶ Have students complete the reproducible "The Land of Counterpane" or the reproducible "Fog."

Day 3

Tips for English Language Learners and Developing Readers

▶ Spend time helping these students understand the terms *symbol* and *symbolism* using items they are familiar with, and gather images from online to show a rose, a red heart, a flag, and a peace sign. Discuss hues that are known to symbolize (white for innocence, black for evil and death); discuss animals that are known to symbolize (dove for peace, owl for wisdom, tiger for strength, and so on).

▶ Find other poems to read and discuss with students and help them identify the symbols and what each means in the context of the poem.

▶ Help those who require it complete the reproducible "Fog."

How I Might Follow Up This Lesson

▶ To help students see figurative language, especially symbolism, as natural to reading, writing, and speaking, I'd provide multiple opportunities for them to discuss poetry and symbolism in narrative and informational texts. Rich discussions can help students clarify authors' meanings and observe diverse interpretations supported with text evidence.

▶ I might ask all or a group of students to compose a poem that uses and develops a symbol. To help students, I'd share several different poems with symbolism (see **www.corwin.com/vocabularyiscomprehension** for more poems).

Juan, a fifth grader whose second language is English, works on visualization before studying symbols. He illustrates fog to show his understanding.

Symbols and Symbolism ("Fog")

NAME: _Juan Jose - Arnulfo_ DATE: _____

"Fog" by Carl Sandburg

The fog comes	1
on little cat feet.	2
It sits looking	3
over harbor and city	4
on silent haunches	5
and then moves on.	6

DIRECTIONS: Read the poem aloud and then silently. Answer the questions using details from the poem.

1. How does the author personify fog? Evaluate this choice.

He used a cat because the cat stays silent.

2. How does personifying the fog help you visualize fog?

the fog is silent and the cat is silent also.

Fifth grader Hayden sees that imagination can make being ill in bed bearable.

Symbols and Symbolism ("Land of Counterpane")

NAME: _Hayden_   DATE: _____

"Land of Counterpane" by Robert Louis Stevenson

When I was sick and lay a-bed,	1
I had two pillows at my head,	2
And all my toys beside me lay,	3
To keep me happy all the day.	4
And sometimes for an hour or so	5
I watched my leaden soldiers go,	6
With different uniforms and drills,	7
Among the bed-clothes, through the hills;	8
And sometimes sent my ships in fleets	9
All up and down among the sheets;	10
Or brought my trees and houses out,	11
And planted cities all about.	12
I was the giant great and still	13
That sits upon the pillow-hill,	14
And sees before him, dale and plain,	15
The pleasant land of counterpane.	16

DIRECTIONS: Read the poem twice and answer the questions using details from the poem.

1. What is a counterpane? What does it symbolize in this poem?

A quilt or blanket a country or land

_____

_____

_____

_____

2. What is the mood or tone of this poem? Use poem details, words, and phrases to support your argument.

The mood is Happy. Its Happy because it says "And all my toys beside me lay, to keep me Happy all the day," and it shows what he does that makes Him Happy.

3. What do the sheets symbolize? Provide supportive details.

The sheets symbolize the ocean. It shows it by saying "I sent my ships in fleets, all up and down the sheets."

Teaching Idioms to English Language Learners

▶ For ELL students to understand lessons taught by teachers and to collaborate and converse with classmates, they need to understand English expressions and idioms. Lessons on idioms should be repeated frequently.

▶ Avoid introducing too many idioms at one time to ELL students so you don't confuse them. Two to three idiomatic expressions a week is enough for the first month. If students show you they can absorb three easily, try introducing four, then five, expressions each week. The sample minilesson on idioms that follows can help you design your own minilessons.

▶ Go to this website to explore more than 3,500 idiomatic expressions: http://www.usingenglish.com/reference/idioms.

Idioms

Goals: In teaching idioms, your aim is to have students catch on to the colorful hodgepodge that is our language and to enjoy learning these figures of speech and where they come from. There is an inherent lighthearted, fun quality to learning idioms, and I find students really enjoy it. They don't even have to catch on that it will give them a serious leg up on comprehension!

An idiom is a group of words that cannot be understood by defining individual words. The idiom has a meaning of its own. Use an idiom such as "out of the blue" to show that its meaning has nothing to do with the color blue. Idioms exist in every language, and their meanings are specific to a culture. Since idiomatic expressions are used in conversations at school and among friends, it important to help students understand and be able to use idiomatic expressions in their conversations.

Materials: Two to five idioms (compose a short conversation for each one), chart paper or whiteboard and markers, copies of the reproducible Idioms for students (see **www.corwin.com/vocabularyiscomprehension** for the reproducible and for the poem "Expressions" by Christina Rossetti)

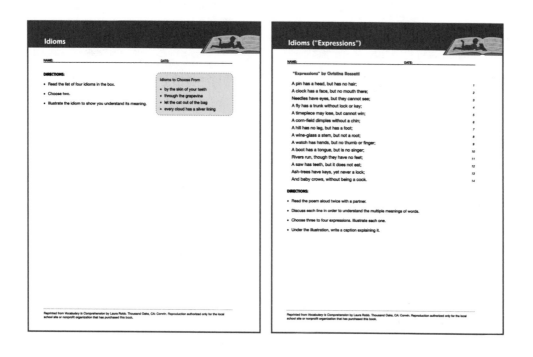

- ▶ Have students tell you what they know about idioms and give examples if possible.
- ▶ Explain idioms to students and offer examples such as *raining cats and dogs, sick as a dog,* and *rub someone the wrong way.*
- ▶ Organize students into pairs.

Day 1

▶ Have students turn to a neighbor and discuss the meanings of the three idioms and offer situations they might use each one. Here are three I use:

  ○ hot under the collar

  ○ head in the clouds

  ○ butterflies in the stomach

> *Here's what fifth graders suggested for "head in the clouds":*
>
> *"Well it doesn't mean that your head is in the sky in the clouds. It means that you dream a lot—you're not on earth but in the clouds." Another pair added, "It's not being practical."*

Day 2

▶ Introduce idioms in a conversation so students can figure out the meaning. Here's what I post on the whiteboard (or write on chart paper) for "get your feet wet."

Amirah: I don't want a speaking part in the play. I'll do sets.

Teacher: Try a small part just to get your feet wet.

Amirah: Can I still do sets?

Teacher: Yes.

▶ Have different partners discuss the meaning of *get your feet wet.*

> *Sixth graders said that it means to try it in a small way to see if you like it. And if you like it, you can do more.*

▶ Have individuals choose two idioms from the first day and use each one in a sentence. Here are the idioms:

  ○ hot under the collar

  ○ head in the clouds

  ○ butterflies in the stomach

▶ Students share the idiom and their sentence with their group.

> *Here are some sentences students created:*
>
> *"Try camping out in your backyard before camping out in the woods to get your feet wet."*
>
> *"Join the community service club for a month to get your feet wet."*
>
> *"Before the test, I had butterflies in my stomach."*
>
> *"I feel butterflies in my stomach every time I have to speak in front of the class."*
>
> *"My mama says I'm always daydreaming and that my head is in the clouds."*
>
> *"My brother says be practical and keep your head out of the clouds."*

Have students choose two idioms introduced by the teacher and write sentences that use these phrases. Then, have students share their sentences with a partner or group.

▶ Give each student a new idiom. Google *idioms*, and you will find websites that you and your students can use.

▶ Organize students into groups of three or four and have students help each other with figuring out the meaning of their idiom.

▶ Introduce each idiom in a conversation starter or a think-aloud and have pairs discuss the idiom or expression. For example, have students discuss when they were jealous of a sibling or friend and include the idiom, *green with envy,* in their discussions.

▶ Have students choose two favorite idioms and draw a scenario that shows the meaning of each one. Cartoons are ideal for this.

▶ Have students complete the reproducible Idioms or Idioms ("Expressions").

How I Might Follow Up This Lesson

▶ I'd want students to use idioms in conversations with their peers. I might give pairs two idioms and ask them to weave the idiom into a conversation. I'd continue to do this until students felt comfortable.

▶ I might ask them to watch the same sitcom on television for several weeks, listen for idiomatic expressions, note the expression on paper, the situation it was spoken in, and what the idiom/expression means.

▶ I would ask students to complete the reproducible "Expressions" by Christina Rossetti.

Using Discussions to Interpret Figurative Language

Discussions can clarify students' understanding of figurative language as well as offer opportunities to listen to peers' interpretations. As students discuss the meanings of figurative language and how the language links to the poem's themes, they deepen comprehension and use the figurative language to visualize (Gambrell, 1996).

Poems should be heard many times and enjoyed for the feelings they raise and for the rhythm of the language. Hearing poetry read aloud can stir deep emotions in readers and is their entrance into the poem's meaning and language. Before asking students to analyze figurative language in a poem, allow students to enjoy the language and imagery by listening (Heard, 1998; Robb, 2013). Use the short poems of Sandra Cisneros and Langston Hughes with developing readers and ELL students because these poems present complex themes and use accessible language.

Poets choose words wisely to express an idea, experience, or emotion. Therefore, studying poetry is the ideal way for students to meet these Common Core craft and structure standards for reading:

▶ Examine words' denotative and connotative meanings and link connotations to the poem's theme and central idea.

▶ Analyze figurative language and visualize ideas while enlarging vocabulary.

▶ Study the impact of rhyme and repetition of sounds such as alliteration, assonance, and consonance on the meaning of a stanza or the entire poem.

▶ Compare themes and central ideas in multiple texts that include poetry along with narratives, memoir, video, charts, and informational texts.

The more students understand and appreciate how figurative language affects a text's imagery and meaning, the more they will enjoy poetry, fiction, and nonfiction.

Build Students' Confidence by Discussing Idioms

From Discussion to Writing
After students have discussed some prompts and/or questions, ask them to write in their readers' notebooks about what they discovered. Moving from talking to writing lets students know what they understand and recall because they can write only what they comprehend.

English language learners benefit from developing an understanding of idiomatic expressions in English. Conversations with peers and adults and among characters in movies, television sitcoms, and videos expect viewers to understand idioms. That's why idioms can be a stumbling block for English language learners because these expressions are a strong part of our oral language. Understanding idioms can help ELL students feel more at ease when conversing with peers and listening to teachers present lessons and facilitate discussions.

Middle grades and middle school are the ideal times for introducing idioms to ELL students who have fluency in English and are ready to study idioms and expressions.

Eventually, these students will include idioms and expressions in their own speech.

Discussions Expand Understanding

Integrating discussions and writing into vocabulary learning leads to a greater understanding of figurative language, connotations, expressions, and word relationships. Students can have discussions with a partner, with a small group, and on a class blog.

Use the guidelines that follow to develop students' enthusiasm for the poems and text that you study. Hopefully, many will choose to read poems independently and find favorite poets whose work they reread again and again.

Open-Ended Prompts and Questions for Discussing Poems and Text Excerpts

Introduce all or some of these questions once students have heard the poem or short text several times and enjoyed it.

- What reactions do you have to the poem or text?

- Are there words whose meanings you need to check?

- Are there key words and phrases that spark connotations? Discuss these.

- What is the poet/author telling you?

- What figurative language do you notice? Explain how each figure of speech adds to the images you build and links to the poem's or test's meaning.

- What questions does the poem/text raise? Discuss these, citing details from the poem or text.

- Is there a stanza, line, or sentence that spoke to you? Share it with your partner and explain why the lines popped out.

- Which words create strong images? Discuss these with your partner.

- Is there repetition? Why do you think the poet/author included these repeated lines or phrases?

- Search for alliteration; assonance, a series of words with similar vowel sounds; and consonance, a series of words with similar consonant sounds, and discuss how the emphasis on consonants and vowels improves your understanding.

- What are some themes in the poem or text? Support your ideas with details from the text or poem.

- Can you pinpoint the central idea(s) and use details from the text or poem to support your thoughts?

Three Reproducibles for Discussing and Writing About Poems

The forms that follow use the open-ended questions above to help students enjoy, relate to, and analyze poems (see **www.corwin.com/vocabularyiscomprehension**).

Dashia explains that Dickinson thinks it's better to be unknown.

Explore a Poem's Meanings

NAME: **Dashia** DATE:

"I'm Nobody" by Emily Dickinson

I'm nobody! Who are you?	1
Are you nobody, too?	2
Then there's a pair of us — don't tell!	3
They'd advertise — you know!	4
How dreary to be somebody!	5
How public like a frog	6
To tell one's name the livelong day	7
To an admiring bog!	8

DIRECTIONS: Read the poem twice and discuss the questions with a partner using details from the poem to support your responses.

- What reactions do you have to the poem or text?
- Are there words whose meanings you need to check?
- Are there key words and phrases that spark connotations? Discuss these.
- Discuss the simile and whether it's effective.
- What are some themes in the poem or text? Support your ideas with details from the text or poem.
- Can you pinpoint the central idea(s) and use details from the text or poem to support your thoughts?

DIRECTIONS: Write your responses below using details from the poem.

1. Explain a theme of this poem and use images and details as support.

She wants to be a nobody and its OK like when she says "there's a pair of us—don't tell!" She wants to be

2. Use images from the poem to state a central idea.

alone and unknown, "How dreary to be a Somebody.

NAME: _____   DATE: _____

"I'm Nobody" by Emily Dickinson

I'm nobody! Who are you?	1
Are you nobody, too?	2
Then there's a pair of us — don't tell!	3
They'd advertise — you know!	4
How dreary to be somebody!	5
How public, like a frog	6
To tell one's name the livelong day	7
To an admiring bog!	8

DIRECTIONS: Read the poem twice and discuss the questions with a partner using details from the poem to support your responses.

• What reactions do you have to the poem or text?

• Are there words whose meanings you need to check?

• Are there key words and phrases that spark connotations? Discuss these.

• Discuss the simile and whether it's effective.

• What are some themes in the poem or text? Support your ideas with details from the text or poem.

• Can you pinpoint the central idea(s) and use details from the text or poem to support your thoughts?

DIRECTIONS: Write your responses below using details from the poem.

1. Explain a theme of this poem and use images and details as support.

2. Use images from the poem to state a central idea.

NAME: _____   DATE: _____

"A Chill" by Christina Rossetti

What can lambkins do	1
All the keen night through?	2
Nestle by their woolly mother	3
The careful ewe.	4
What can nestlings do	5
In the nightly dew?	6
Sleep beneath their mother's wing	7
Till day breaks anew.	8
If in a field or tree	9
There might only be	10
Such a warm soft sleeping-place	11
Found for me!	12

DIRECTIONS: Read the poem twice and discuss the questions with a partner using details from the poem to support your responses.

- What are your first reactions to the poem or text?

- Are there words whose meanings you need to check?

- Are there key words and phrases that spark connotations? Discuss these.

- What is the poet/author telling you?

- Which words create strong images? Discuss these with your partner.

DIRECTIONS: Write your responses below using details from the poem.

1. Explain why the poem is called "A Chill."

2. How do the images of the first two stanzas help you understand the third stanza?

NAME: _____   DATE: _____

"No Man Is an Island" by John Donne

No man is an island,	1
Entire of itself,	2
Everyman is a piece of the continent,	3
A part of the main.	4
If a clod be washed away by the sea,	5
Europe is the less.	6
As well as if a promontory were.	7
As well as if a manor of thy friend's	8
Or of thine own were:	9
Any man's death diminishes me,	10
Because I am involved in mankind,	11
And therefore never send to know for whom the bell tolls;	12
It tolls for thee.	13

DIRECTIONS: Read the poem twice and discuss the questions with a partner using details from the poem to support your responses.

- What is the poet/author telling you?

- What figurative language do you notice? Explain how each figure of speech adds to the images you build and links to the poem's or text's meaning.

- What questions does the poem/text raise? Discuss these citing details from the poem or text.

- Is there a stanza, line, or sentence that spoke to you? Share it with your partner and explain why the lines popped out.

- Which words create strong images? Discuss these with your partner.

DIRECTIONS: Write your responses below using details from the poem.

1. Explain the meaning of "No Man Is an Island" using the connotations associated with island and the examples in Donne's poem.

2. Connect the phrase "never send to know for whom the bell tolls" to the title.

Discussions on Class Blogs

In addition to traditional whole-class discussions, it's fun for students to discuss a poem on a class blog. Students can do so in pairs, small groups—mix it up. The benefit of these types of discussions is that teachers can read students' exchanges and ask thought-provoking, follow-up questions. I find that reading students discussions provides me with a clear picture of students' strengths and needs. It's also easy to spot who is not participating, and meet one-to-one to find out what is holding him or her back from contributing to the discussion. Mix traditional discussions with discussions on a class blog. One group can log onto your class blog and discuss; the remaining groups complete traditional discussions.

Here is an excerpt along with my observations from a conversation on a class blog about an Emily Dickinson poem (see box on page 107). This discussion among Mara, Jesse, Roberto, and RaShawyn focused on personification and denotative and connotative meanings of words students selected.

> "Prodigious means abnormal here—that's the literal meaning. But I also think of extraordinary moves, marvelous and amazing, too." (Mara)

> "I think the word peers—that's personification because a train can't peer and supercilious tells what kind of peering—as if the train was snooty, proud, looking down at shanties." (Roberto)

> "You're right, Roberto. Especially 'cause shanties are poor houses, so the train seems to look down on these." (RaShawyn)

> "What about Boanerges?" (Roberto)

> "I got it. [Uses online dictionary.] Says it's a nickname that Jesus used for the Apostles James and John. It also says a preacher with a powerful voice." (Mara)

> "Cool." (Jesse)

> "I think Boanerges helps hear the sound the train makes—it's strong and powerful and heard for miles." (RaShawyn)

Robb's Observations

The group continues to blog about the oxymoron, docile and omnipotent, and Robert gets that "Boanerges" is an allusion. I immediately notice that Jesse's sole contribution to the blog is "cool." I might not have picked this up in traditional discussions as four to five occur at the same time, and it's difficult to monitor all students. Partner and group discussions on blogs tap into students' love of social media and at the same time provide me with insights into who participated and the quality of each student's contributions.

In a follow-up conference with Jesse, I asked him, "Why didn't you enter in the discussion?" His first response was "Dunno."

The next day during a short second conference, Jesse answered my question: "I'm bad with words and meanings. I don't want to look dumb." Jesse's silence was a coping strategy. Instead of placing Jesse in a group, I had him work with a partner and gave the pair poems that had a few challenging words so they didn't feel overwhelmed. In addition, I frequently listened to Jesse and his partner, taking every opportunity to praise both for their thinking and ability to connect a figure of speech to the poem's meaning. Besides enlarging Jesse's vocabulary, I worked on building his self-confidence so he would risk answering in a group or before the entire class. I reported Jesse's comments to his content teachers to make them aware of his need for extra vocabulary support and his reluctance to participate.

"I Like to See It Lap the Miles"
by Emily Dickinson

I like to see it lap the Miles—	1
And lick the Valleys up—	2
And stop to feed itself at Tanks—	3
And then—prodigious step	4
Around a Pile of Mountains—	5
And supercilious peer	6
In Shanties—by the sides of Roads—	7
And then a Quarry pare	8
To fit its sides	9
And crawl between	10
Complaining all the while	11
In horrid—hooting stanza—	12
Then chase itself down Hill—	13
And neigh like Boanerges—	14
Then—prompter than a Star	15
Stop—docile and omnipotent	16
At its own stable door—	17

Collaborate and Learn

1. With a colleague or a small group of colleagues, investigate and discuss the following websites on idioms. How might you integrate using the websites into lessons for ELL students?

   http://www.englishclub.com/ref/Idioms/A/index.htm

   http://www.idiomsite.com/

   http://www.learnenglishfeelgood.com/americanidioms/

2. Plan with a peer partner some minilessons for figurative language. (Besides the excerpts from poems in this chapter, you'll find other poems you can use at **www.corwin.com/vocabularyiscomprehension**).

3. Share the poems with other members of your team.

4. Try blogging about figurative language with a small group so you can experience how blogging can deepen your understanding of figurative language.

5. Discuss why it's important to have rich conversations about figurative language in texts and why these discussions can improve comprehension and build vocabulary.

Getting to the Root of Words

I t's rare in language arts teaching when we can say with mathematical precision how much a student can learn in the space of a few weeks. But when it comes to teaching the roots of words, we *can* quantify our expectations and goals. How is this possible? Because *about 90 percent* of English words of two or more syllables are of Greek or Latin origin. This is one of the most underutilized truths in language arts instruction. If we can harness the power of these Greek and Latin roots to crack open the meaning of 90 percent of the English language for students, think about the implications for achievement.

Where to begin this work? It's like the adage, "Yard by yard it's hard, but inch by inch it's a cinch." Take on a small group of roots one at a time. For example, the seventh-grade team at Daniel Morgan Middle School in Winchester, Virginia, developed a cross-curricular root word study plan for the first quarter of school (see following chart). In nine weeks, seventh graders studied thirty-six roots along with prefixes and suffixes and created around 360 words. Sixth- and eighth-grade teams at the school have also prepared cross-curricular lists of roots that apply to topics students read and study. This means that students can understand the meanings of 1,080 words in nine weeks as well as build the multiple forms of each word.

And another example: Take the four most common prefixes—*un-, re-, in-, dis-*. When you teach these prefixes and students know them well, it opens them up to easily knowing 1,500 word meanings. Clearly, teaching roots is an extremely efficient way to expand students' general academic and domain-specific vocabulary in a relatively short period of time. In doing so, we also provide them with the tools that can improve their ability to use prefixes, suffixes, and roots to decode compound and multisyllable words.

WEEK	ROOT/PREFIX	ORIGIN	MEANING
QUARTER 1	CIVICS AND ECONOMICS		
1	civ-, civi-	Latin	citizen
2	demo-	Greek	people
3	crat-	Greek	power
4	leg-	Latin	law
5	bi-	Latin	two
6	soci-, socio-	Latin	to join, companions
7	crimin-	Latin	to judge
8	loc-	Latin	area, place
9	corpus-	Latin	body
QUARTER 2	MATH		
1	uni-	Latin	one
2	mono-	Latin	one, single
3	tri-	Greek and Latin	three
4	quad-, quart-	Greek and Latin	four
5	poly-	Greek	many
6	centi-	Latin	hundred
7	trans-	Latin	across
8	equ-, equi-	Latin	equal
9	cycl-	Latin	circle
QUARTER 3	ENGLISH		
1	viv-, vit-	Latin	live
2	cred-	Latin	believe
3	pel-	Latin	drive or push
4	spec-	Latin	to see or to look
5	vert-	Latin	turn
6	therm-	Greek	heat
7	aut-	Greek	self
8	cast-	Old English	to throw out or calculate
9	pend-	Latin	hang
QUARTER 4	SCIENCE		
1	hydro-	Greek	water
2	geo-	Greek	earth
3	chromo-	Greek	color
4	hyper-	Greek	over
5	hypo-	Greek	under
6	endo-	Greek	inside
7	ecto-	Modern Latin	outside
8	derma	Modern Latin	skin
9	pseudo-	Late Latin	false

A seventh grade cross-curricular list of Latin and Greek roots, stems, and prefixes for word study from Daniel Morgan Middle School.

What the Common Core State Standards Have to Say

The Common Core Vocabulary Standard 4b states, "Use common, grade-appropriate Greek or Latin affixes and roots as clues to the meaning of a word." Studying roots and affixes across the curriculum is an efficient way to enlarge students' vocabulary. The study of one root along with prefixes and suffixes can lead to an understanding of 10 or more words related to that root.

In Standard 6, the Common Core requires that students "acquire and use accurately grade-appropriate general academic and domain-specific words and phrases." By building words using Greek and Latin roots, prefixes, and suffixes, students can improve their comprehension of academic vocabulary and develop fluency with 90 percent of the words that appear in texts for Grades 3 to 9 (Blachowicz, Fisher, Ogle, & Watts-Taffe, 2006; Berne & Blachowicz, 2009; Kieffer & Lesaux, 2007; Rasinski, Padak, & Newton, 2008).

Ultimately, improved general academic and domain-specific vocabulary leads to students' ability to read and comprehend grade-level complex texts. The most effective way to teach vocabulary is to select and teach roots that relate to topics in English, social studies, science, and mathematics. In this chapter, I show you how to go about this word study systematically, with the 10- to 15-minutes-a-day approach outlined in previous chapters.

Definitions to Share With Students

Prefix: A prefix is a letter or a small group of letters that have meaning and are attached to the beginning of a word. Prefixes change the meaning of a root or a base word. For example, *connect* is a base word that means to join; add the prefix *dis—disconnect—* and now the word means the opposite of connect—to sever or interrupt.

Base Word: A base word is a word that can stand on its own; it's the word without any prefixes or suffixes. For example, *call* is the base word, but *recall* and *caller* aren't base words because one contains the prefix *re* and the other the suffix *er*.

Root: A root is the form of a word after the prefixes and suffixes have been removed. Unlike a base word, the root cannot function as a word on its own. For example, in*jus-tice* is from the root *jus* and *incredible* is from the root *cred*.

Suffix: A suffix is a word ending that can come after a root or base word. Suffixes usually indicate a word's part of speech. For example, *exclaim* is a verb and adding *ation—exclamation—*turns it into a noun.

Affixes: An affix is a word element, usually a prefix and suffix, that can be attached to the beginning or end of a base word or root.

Review Lessons on Prefixes and Suffixes

If your students know little about prefixes and suffixes, set aside two 15-minute lessons on consecutive days to teach them how these terms support figuring out the meanings of words.

Lesson 2 in Chapter 2 on pages 22–25 introduces prefixes and suffixes and roots as aids to decoding (e.g., multisyllable words), and encoding (exploring meaning). If your students did well with this lesson, then consider skipping these review lessons on prefixes and suffixes.

Prefixes

Goals: Prefixes attached to the beginning of a root or base word change the word's meaning. It's beneficial to learn prefixes and their meanings because this will enable your students to determine the literal meaning of unfamiliar words as they read grade-level, complex texts.

Materials: This lesson uses the base word *connect*. Copies of student handout Twenty Most Common Prefixes (see **www.corwin.com/ vocabularyiscomprehension**)

Twenty Most Common Prefixes

PREFIX	MEANING	EXAMPLE
anti	against	antiaircraft
de	opposite	deport
*dis	not, opposite of	disappear
en, em	cause to	enclose, embalm
fore	before	foretell
in, im	in	infect, immediate
*in, im, il, ir	not	irregular
inter	between	international
mid	middle	midpoint
mis	wrongly	misunderstood
non	not	nonexistent
over	over	oversee
pre	before	prefix
re	again	restate
semi	half	semicircle
sub	under	subterranean
super	above	superhuman
trans	across	transmigrate
*un	not	undeveloped
*under	under	underachiever

Note: The * before prefixes means that they account for 97% of words with prefixes in school texts.

Reprinted from *Vocabulary Is Comprehension* by Laura Robb. Thousand Oaks, CA: Corwin. Reproduction authorized only for the local school site or nonprofit organization that has purchased this book.

Day 1

▶ Organize students into pairs.

▶ Give each student a copy of the prefix handout.

▶ Write the word *connect* on the chalkboard. Have partners discuss its meaning.

{ *Fourth graders say* connect *means to bring together, to join, to tie or tape.*

▶ Ask students to use the prefixes *dis* and *re* to build new words using *connect*.

▶ Have partners discuss how *dis—disconnect—*and *re—reconnect—*alter the meaning of connect.

{ *After looking up the meanings of* dis *and* re *on their prefix handout, a pair of fourth graders said that* dis *means not and* disconnect *means not connected. Another pair explained that* re *means again and* reconnect *means to hook up again.*

Day 2

▶ Continue practicing with other words if the class or a group needs it. Some words you might use are *just, ordinary, function, exclude,* and *term.*

Suffixes

Goals: To help students understand that suffixes are at the end of a word and can reveal a word's part of speech or the tense of a verb.

Materials: This lesson uses the word *connect*. Copies of student handout Twenty Most Common Suffixes (see **www.corwin.com/vocabularyiscomprehension**)

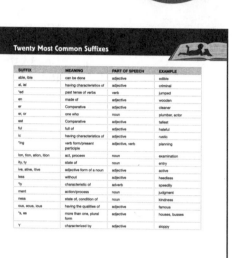

Twenty Most Common Suffixes

SUFFIX	MEANING	PART OF SPEECH	EXAMPLE
able, ible	can be done	adjective	edible
al, ial	having characteristics of	adjective	criminal
*ed	past tense of verbs	verb	jumped
en	made of	adjective	wooden
er	Comparative	adjective	cleaner
er, or	one who	noun	plumber, actor
est	Comparative	adjective	tallest
ful	full of	adjective	hateful
ic	having characteristics of	adjective	rustic
*ing	verb form/present participle	adjective, verb	planning
ion, tion, ation, ition	act, process	noun	examination
ity, ty	state of	noun	entry
ive, ative, itive	adjective form of a noun	adjective	active
less	without	adjective	heedless
*ly	characteristic of	adverb	speedily
ment	action/process	noun	judgment
ness	state of, condition of	noun	kindness
ous, eous, ious	having the qualities of	adjective	famous
*s, es	more than one, plural form	adjective	houses, busses
Y	characterized by	adjective	sloppy

*Note: The * before suffixes means that they account for 97% of words with suffixes in school texts.*

Reprinted from Vocabulary Is Comprehension by Laura Robb. Thousand Oaks, CA: Corwin. Reproduction authorized only for the local school site or nonprofit organization that has purchased this book.

> ▸ Organize students into groups of four.

> ▸ Give each student a copy of the suffix handout.

> ▸ Ask group members to collaborate and add *tion, able, or, er, ed,* and *ing* to *connect.*

Day 1

Fourth graders offered these words: connection, connectable, connector, connecter, connected, connecting.

> ▸ Ask group members to find the parts of speech each suffix indicates using their suffix handout.

> ▸ Ask groups to share what they discover about parts of speech and record it on chart paper or a whiteboard.

Here's what students discovered: tion, *a noun;* able, *an adjective;* er *and* or, *nouns;* ed, *past tense;* ing, *present tense.*

> ▸ Continue practicing with other words if the class or a group needs it. Some words you might use are *resist, annoy, deceive, convert,* and *involve.*

Day 2

A Five-Day Routine for Teaching Roots

To teach roots and affixes, plan to spend about 10 to 15 minutes a day, each school day. Wrap up each lesson by asking students to complete a reproducible, as doing so really helps them "own" what you just covered as a class. On the sixth day, help students see the connections between what they are learning in a unit and the root being studied (see pages 122–123). I've included a set of lessons presented in sixth-grade English class using the roots *viv* and *vit* that relates to their unit on survival. The structure of the daily lessons is the same for English, social studies, and mathematics and follows the minilesson framework presented in Chapter 1 on page 8.

Selecting the Roots

To select a root to teach, it's ideal to choose one that relates to the topic, such as *revolution* in history or *survival* in English or reading workshop. You also want to take into consideration the entire unit, not just one short complex text, so that students have opportunities to spot the root in multiple texts and contexts. For example, for a sixth-grade unit on *survival*, I start with the roots *viv* and *vit*. As students read the assigned texts, I tell them to be on the lookout for words related to *viv* and *vit* and jot the word in their readers' notebooks.

In the course of a 5-week unit, sixth graders read a novel, an informational text, and an article at their instructional reading levels. A few groups watched videos (see the box on pages 121–122 for a list of possible students' learning resources).

When the 5-day study of *viv* and *vit* ended, I asked students to share some words they found in their reading materials and continued to have them share words at the end of each week until the unit ended.

Teaching students Greek and Latin roots, along with common prefixes and suffixes, is a gateway to understanding 90 percent of words in the English language.

Expand Vocabulary With Roots, Prefixes, and Suffixes

Goals: The study of roots, prefixes, and suffixes across the curriculum exposes students to the general academic and domain-specific words they'll continually meet in their reading. In this model minilesson from a unit on survival, students experience firsthand what it's like to learn a root and then build words to support their reading, writing, and speaking. Here, they find words that derive from the Latin roots *vit* and *viv*. Additionally, the minilesson demonstrates how knowing prefixes, suffixes, and roots can help readers figure out the literal or denotative meanings of words.

Materials: Chart paper and markers or a computer and whiteboard, copies of reproducibles Words in Different Situations and Related or Unrelated (see **www .corwin.com/vocabularyiscomprehension**)

Words in Different Situations

NAME: _____ DATE: _____

DIRECTIONS:

Below is a word and three different situations in which one might use the word.

• Use the word and situation in a sentence.

• Explain, under each sentence, how the word's meaning changes in each situation.

Word: revitalize

SITUATION 1: A DROOPING PLANT

_____

_____

_____

SITUATION 2: DRY OR UNRULY HAIR

_____

_____

_____

SITUATION 3: A FISH TANK

_____

_____

_____

Reprinted from *Vocabulary Is Comprehension* by Laura Robb. Thousand Oaks, CA: Corwin. Reproduction authorized only for the local school site or nonprofit organization that has purchased this book.

Related or Unrelated

NAME: _____ DATE: _____

DIRECTIONS:

• Read the list of words below and decide which is related to the root *port*, meaning to carry.

• Check an online or print dictionary to determine which words are related to the root *port* and which aren't related.

• Put the words in the box on the chart where they belong.

Words: porter, important, export, transportation, portent, deport, portion, import, report, portable, portly, transport, portrait

WORDS FROM PORT THAT MEAN "TO CARRY"	WORDS THAT DON'T MEAN "TO CARRY"

Reprinted from *Vocabulary Is Comprehension* by Laura Robb. Thousand Oaks, CA: Corwin. Reproduction authorized only for the local school site or nonprofit organization that has purchased this book.

Day 1

▶ Write on chart paper or project onto a whiteboard, the root, the language it derives from, and its meaning.

    vit, viv   Latin   means live; life

▶ Model the process of coming up with a word based on the root. Here's what I say:

First, I say the root aloud and then its meaning—live, life—to see if pronouncing these words helps me think of words. Sur<u>viv</u>al, for sure, and that's the theme we are studying. I know the word *vital*, which means lively, full of energy. I wonder if lively comes from *viv*? I'll have to look that up. What other situations come to mind when I think of survival and the idea of being in an extreme fight for life or energy? Let me try adding a common prefix to see if I can find more words. *Re-vive*. Yes, that's a word meaning to bring back. *Vit*—what words begin with that?

▶ Organize students into partners. Tell them you want them to do the same kind of thinking and wondering that you modeled—saying the roots aloud to see if they spark related words, trying prefixes, and so on.

▶ To help students who have no suggestions for words that relate to *viv* and *vit* write these questions on the board:

  ○ What pills do some people take for health?

  ○ What's a word for an extremely bright color or scene?

  ○ For the life of the party?

  ○ Can you find multiple forms of *survive* and *revive*?

▶ Have students pair-share for two minutes and generate words they think come from the roots *viv*, *vit*.

▶ Project an online dictionary on the whiteboard if the questions don't help students generate words and discuss several with students.

▶ Invite pairs to share their words.

▶ Record words on chart paper or project onto the whiteboard.

Building a Bank of Resources
On the Corwin website (**www .corwin.com/vocabularyis comprehension**), you'll find a list of Greek and Latin roots as well as a list of prefixes and suffixes. By Googling any of the three terms, you can find additional roots, prefixes, and suffixes for the discipline you teach.

The sixth graders' list of words for roots *viv* and *vit*.

vital	vitality
survive	revive
survival	revival

Day 2

▶ Read aloud the list of words collected on the first day and ask students to pair-share to see if they can generate more words for the roots *viv* and *vit*.

▶ Record the words that students added on the class chart or whiteboard.

The list of words sixth-grade students generated on the first and second days.

revitalize	reviving
revived	reviver
survivor	vitamin
vivacious	vivid
vivisection	vitals
survive	surviving
survived	invite (not from the root, vit)
vital	

▶ Explain that students can challenge a word if they doubt that a word came from the root beings studied. (See **www.corwin.com/vocabularyiscomprehension**

for the reproducible Related or Unrelated, which asks students to check out words to see if they do or don't come from a specific root.)

▶ Research each challenge in a dictionary. For *vit*, students challenged *invite* saying, "It has *vit* in it, but it doesn't connect to the meaning live or life."

▶ Look up the challenged word in an online or print dictionary and flash it onto a whiteboard or use a print dictionary and place it under a document camera for students to see. *Invite* comes from the French word *inviter* and the Latin word *invitare*, both meaning to make a request. Therefore, invite does not come from the root *vit*.

▶ Help students understand that even though a word contains the root, it's important to consider the word's meaning, and *invite* does not relate to the meaning of *vit*—live, life.

▶ Organize students into pairs.

▶ Ask pairs to use their knowledge of the roots *viv* and *vit* and prefixes and suffixes to define all the words the class generated. Following is the list of words with students' definitions for words that come from the roots *viv*, *vit*.

▶ Have students compile a list of prefixes used in these words and their definitions in a section of their readers' notebooks reserved for vocabulary. Students can use online or print dictionaries to help them define each prefix.

Word(s)	Definition
revitalize	to mend, to breathe new life into
revive, revived, reviving	to bring to life again
reviver	a person who brings someone back to life again
survive, survived, surviving	to be able to live and stay alive
survivor	a person who makes it through a tough experience
vital	needed for living
vitals	body signs such as heartbeat and blood pressure that show health
vitamin	a pill that makes you healthy
vivacious	full of life and energy
vivisection	operations on living animals to study their organs and diseases
vivid	brightly colored, lively

Sixth-grade students define words using prefixes, suffixes, and the roots.

▶ As a class, read aloud the definitions completed on the third day, and have students refine or adjust those that need tweaking. At this point, students can use online or print dictionaries for support.

▶ Discuss with students the various situations in which a word is often used, and contribute suggestions if students have difficulty. Add situations to the chart completed on the third day.

▶ Select one to three words, and model how the situation enables you to compose a sentence that highlights your understanding of the word. Have students discuss the variations in the word's meaning when the context or situation changes.

Word(s)	Definition	Situations
revitalize	to mend, to breathe new life into	giving CPR, an operation, regular exercise, special diet
revive, revived, reviving	to bring to life again	after cardiac arrest, after almost drowning, after surgery
reviver	a person who brings someone back to life again	doctor, lifeguard, fireman, first responder, person who knows CPR
survive, survived, surviving	to be able to live and stay alive	emotional survival; in extreme hardship like no food, limited water; surviving abuse or an attack
survivor	a person who makes it through a tough experience	any tough experience, operation, hiking, snake bite, thirst
vital	needed for living	water, food shelter, family, education
vitals	body signs such as heartbeat and blood pressure that show health	taken by a nurse, doctor, physician assistant; diabetes pump
vitamin	a pill that makes you healthy	daily doses of vitamins, calcium for bones, vitamin D prevents rickets, for health
vivacious	full of life and energy	person's actions at a party, in a group, or on stage; personality type
vivisection	operations on living animals to study their organs and diseases	medical research, cosmetic industry, food industry
vivid	brightly colored, lively	rainbow, painting, clothing, hair color

With the teacher's support, students assign situations for each word.

▶ Next, compose two or three sample sentences that reveal an understanding of one of the word's meaning and functions in different contexts. Modeling and then having students write their own sentences is a powerful way to further students' connection to the word and their understanding of its nuances. Here are the three sentences the teacher wrote in front of his sixth-grade class. If the class or a small group needs additional modeling, do the same process with another word.

1. The sailor <u>survived</u> a four-day ordeal at sea in a rubber lifeboat because he rationed water and food supplies.

2. The crystal vase <u>survived</u> being mailed from Seattle to New York.

3. Her hands <u>survived</u> washing dishes for two hours in hot water only when she bathed them in soothing lotion.

▶ Organize students into pairs.

▶ Have pairs select two to six words and use each word in a sentence that reflects an understanding of the word. Tier this task by inviting students at different reading levels to write the number of sentences appropriate for them.

▶ Ask partners to share their sentences with the class by entering them into the teacher's computer and projecting them onto a whiteboard or writing them on the chalkboard.

Day 5

▶ Have students complete one or two of the reproducibles.

Day 6

Tips for English Language Learners and Developing Readers

▶ Provide support on the day students write sentences.

▶ Help pairs who can write sentences select words they understand.

▶ Work one-to-one with students who can come to understand the process with you, offering scaffolds such as the following:

○ Compose sentences orally and then have the students write their own sentences.

○ Discuss a specific situation and what a sentence might look like, and then ask the student to say the sentence out loud before writing it. Support comes from the spoken sentence.

○ Invite students to reinforce their knowledge of roots and affixes by completing the charts on this website: http://www.readwritethink.org/files/resources/lesson_images/lesson1042/game_chart.pdf.

Make Words With Prefixes, Suffixes, and Roots

Goals: Once students know several prefixes and roots and they understand that the prefix changes the word's meaning, it's time to turbocharge their word acquisition by having them build many words using sets of prefixes, roots, and suffixes. For this sample lesson, I've included a set of prefixes, suffixes, and roots for students (see **www .corwin.com/vocabularyiscomprehension**). I encourage you to use this set to devise other fun games for your students.

Materials: Copies of the reproducible Make Words With Prefixes, Suffixes, and Roots for each student (see **www.corwin.com/vocabularyiscomprehension**) and chart paper or whiteboard

Day 1

▸ Organize students in pairs.

▸ Explain that the goal of this challenge is to make as many words as possible in seven to eight minutes. Words can have a prefix and root, a root and a suffix, or a prefix, root, and suffix.

▸ Ask partners to work together and create as many real words as possible.

▸ Have partners join another pair to form a group of four. Have students exchange words and add new words to their lists.

Day 2

▸ Ask students to work in the same groups.

▸ Have group members check any doubtful words in an online or print dictionary before sharing with the class.

▸ Note the words students share on chart paper or project them onto a whiteboard.

▸ Work with and offer support to English language learners and developing readers who at this point in their development lack the skill to work with a partner.

Prefix	Root	Suffix
a, an, ad, af, ag, ar, ac, at	belli (war)	er, or
dis, dif, di	fract (part)	sion, tion
re	tract (pull)	able, ible

Prefix	Root	Suffix
sub	spect (look)	ence, ance
in	dem (people)	ure
de	meter (measure)	late
intro	port (carry)	tude
im	scrib (write)	ous
trans	narr (tell)	ate
con		ive

Make words with prefixes, suffixes, and roots.

Choosing Texts for Units

Below is a list of books you might consider for a unit on survival. They comprise diverse reading levels, something you always want for your class. You can also use Google to find videos and articles on survival at a variety of reading levels. Having reading materials at a range of complexity is the make-or-break factor in meeting students' needs. Motivation and engagement occur when students can easily read and learn from texts, contribute to discussions, and collaborate on projects.

Literature: Fiction

- *A Long Walk to Water: Based on a True Story* by Linda Sue Park, HMH Books for Young Readers, 2011
- *Hatchet* by Gary Paulsen, Simon & Shuster, 2006
- *Inside Out & Back Again* by Thanhha Lai, HarperCollins, 2013
- *Lyddie* by Katherine Paterson, Puffin, 2004
- *So Far From the Bamboo Grove* by Yoko Kawashima Watkins, HarperCollins, 2008
- *Life of Pi* by Yann Martel, Mariner Books, 2003
- *Shiloh* by Phyllis Reynolds Naylor, Aladdin, 2000
- *The Friendship* by Mildred Taylor, Puffin, 1998
- *The Gold Cadillac* by Mildred Taylor, Puffin, 1998
- *Forging Freedom: A True Story of the Holocaust* by Hudson Talbot, Putnam, 2000

Informational Texts: Nonfiction

- *Blizzard!* by Jim Murphy, Scholastic, 2000
- *The Great Fire* by Jim Murphy, Scholastic, 2010
- *When the Plague Strikes: The Black Death, Smallpox, AIDS* by James Cross Giblin, HarperCollins, 1997
- *Zlata's Diary: A Child's Life in Wartime Sarajevo* by Zlata Filipovec, Penguin, 2006
- *Years of Dust: The Story of the Dust Bowl* by Albert Marin, Puffin, 2012
- *Freedom Walkers: The Story of the Montgomery Bus Boycott*, by Russell Freedman, Holiday House, 2008

(Continued)

(Continued)

Picture Books

- *Sixteen Years in Sixteen Seconds: The Sammy Lee Story* by Paula Yoo, Lee & Low, 2005
- *The Worst of Friends: Thomas Jefferson, John Adams, and the True Story of an American Feud* by Susanne Tripp Jumain, Dutton Juvenile, 2011
- *The Hickory Chair* by Lisa Rowe Faustino, Scholastic, 2001
- *The True Story of Ruby Bridges* by Robert Coles, Scholastic, 2010
- *Through My Eyes* by Ruby Bridges, Scholastic, 1999
- *Landed* by Milly Lee, Farrar, Straus & Giroux, 2006
- *Sparrow Girl* by Sara Pennypacker, Disney-Hyperion, 2009
- *Survival at 40 Below* by Debbie S. Miller, Walker, 2012
- *Richard Wright and the Library Card* by William Miller, Lee & Low, 1997
- *Under the Quilt of Night* by Deborah Hopkinson, Aladdin, 2005

How to Link the Lessons to Students' Reading

After completing the week's worth of lessons on the root that introduces your unit of study, invite students to find words related to the theme or topic from their reading and from watching videos. For example, on the unit on survival, which lasted 5 weeks, students shared words from their independent reading and viewing at the end of each week. The beauty of connecting word study to students' independent reading and digital viewing is that you dramatically widen the "fishnet" that gets cast. Students come upon related words in all sorts of authentic contexts and bring them back to class for sharing. The words go far beyond words related to *viv* and *vit*. And to deepen the assignment further, I ask students not only to list words from their reading in their readers' notebooks but also explain the connection to the word *survival*. (Note: If words came from a book, students noted the title, author, and page number; if words came from a video, students noted its title.)

Sharing the Collection Each Friday

At the end of the week (or Monday if you prefer) collect students' words on chart paper or a whiteboard, and note the title of the book or video the words were from so you can jot down words under specific titles each time students share. Use the 15 to 20 minutes set aside for daily vocabulary instruction for the entire class to discuss the words and connect each one to the unit's topic or theme. This is a great investment of learning time because all students, by listening to classmates, have opportunities to expand their vocabulary. If there's extra available time, you can explore roots related to words that students have found.

Here's the list of words related to survival that sixth graders found in *Hatchet* by Gary Paulson, *Blizzard!* by Jim Murphy, and *Landed* by Milly Lee halfway through the unit. You'll notice how rich and varied the words are. One student did not cull all the words that follow; the lists resulted from several students reading the same book at different points in the unit.

Invite students to think about the lesson on root words by asking them to find words related to the lesson in their reading.

Some Survival-Related Words From *Hatchet*: *overcome, agony, slew, raged, wreck, extensive searches, motivated, gear, gingerly, ignite, exasperation, dormant, convulse, bait, vital, devastating, stabilize, refine, frenzied*

Some Survival-Related Words From *Blizzard!* *storm, velocity, anemometer, fatigue, ferocity, violent shift of wind, churning waves, rescues, drifts, hypothermia, ordeal, blizzard, exhaustion, sheer determination, fierce wind, struggled and clawed, marooned, clogged, hike, pushed and pounded, floundered, shelter, numbing cold, raw power*

Some Survival-Related Words From *Landed*: *interrogated, sent back, remember with maps, house plans, charts, worries, identification card, disembark, flushed with humiliation, direction, compass, landed*

More Strategies That Use Roots, Prefixes, and Suffixes

The lessons in this next section are whole-class lessons that engage 25 to 30-plus students in the activity because a large group will generate an extensive list of words. The more words students suggest, the more words they can learn. In addition, you'll find that as you reread a list of words that students suggested, you'll notice that you have a combination of general academic and domain-specific vocabulary (Larson, Dixon, & Townsend, 2013).

LESSON 5

Prefix Brainstorm

Make Words With Prefixes

NAME: _____ DATE: _____

DIRECTIONS: Working with a partner, complete the following tasks.

• Select a prefix from the box below.

RE	IN, IM	UN	CON	DE	MIS	AB	PRE

• Think of words that start with this prefix and write them in the space provided. You can use an online or print dictionary to identify other words to add to your lists.

WORD	OTHER FORMS OF THE WORD

Reprinted from *Vocabulary Is Comprehension* by Laura Robb. Thousand Oaks, CA: Corwin. Reproduction authorized only for the local school site or nonprofit organization that has purchased this book.

Goals: Using a prefix to brainstorm a list of words can yield a variety of words. Next, students can identify words that have multiple forms—*survive, survived, surviving, survival, survivor*—and share these with the class. Use the handout Twenty Most Common Prefixes (see **www.corwin.com/vocabularyiscomprehension**) and start with the starred prefixes as these begin the most words.

Materials: Paper and pencils, chart paper or whiteboard, a specific prefix, copies of reproducible Make Words With Prefixes (see **www .corwin.com/vocabularyiscomprehension**)

Day 1

▶ Organize students into pairs.

▶ Explain that partners will have 15 minutes to create a list in their readers' notebooks of words that start with the prefix.

▶ Encourage pairs to talk and write, talk and write to generate as many words as possible in 15 minutes.

Day 2

▶ Compile each pairs' words on chart paper or project them onto a whiteboard.

▶ Invite students to reread the list and offer words to add to the list.

▶ Divide words among partners and have them discuss meanings and everything they know about each word.

▶ Lead a whole-class sharing of what students know about the words.

▶ Check in an online dictionary to clarify meanings or find multiple meanings. For example, *disentangle* can refer to untangling hair; freeing oneself from involvement in a club, organization, or relationship; or unraveling a knot in a chain, shoelace, or rope.

Day 3

▶ Organize students into groups of four.

- Think aloud and model how you generate words that start with the prefix *dis*.

- Give each group a column or a specific number of words to list multiple forms of a word. The teacher collects these and writes them on chart paper or projects them onto a whiteboard.

- Have students complete the reproducible.

Tips for English Language Learners and Developing Readers

- Have English language learners (ELLs) with limited English ability and developing readers who are several years below grade level work with you to try to generate a few words.

- Help these students understand that they can gain much by observing the generation of words and discussion of their meanings.

Day 4

Multiple Forms of Words From Prefix *dis*

dislike, disliked, disliking

disenchanted, disenchant, disenchanting

disarm, disarmed, disarming, disarmament

dissect, dissected, dissecting, dissection

dislike	disenchanted	disentangled	disbelief
disoriented	disrespect	disinherit	disable
disabuse	disadvantage	disaggregate	disallow
disappear	disapprove	disarmament	disarm
disarray	disassociate	disentangle	disavow
disband	disbar	disbursed	discern
discharge	disclaim	disclose	discomfort
discontinue	discord	discourage	discount
discourteous	discredit	disdain	disunite
disembody	disengage	disfigure	disgrace
disguise	disgorge	disharmony	dishonor
disinclined	disinfect	disinterest	dislocation
dislodged	dismantle	dismembered	dismount
disobedient	disorderly	disorganized	disowned
dispensation	displeasure	disprove	disputer
disqualify	disquiet	disrobe	disrupt
dissatisfy	dissect	dissemble	dissent
dissimilar	distasteful	distortion	distract

Students see the wealth of words that begin with the prefix *dis*.

Denotation-Connotation Map

Denotative and Connotative Meanings of Words

NAME: _____ DATE: _____

"To Make a Prairie" by Emily Dickinson

To make a prairie it takes a clover and one bee—
One clover, and a bee,
And revery.
The revery alone will do
If bees are few.

DIRECTIONS:

- Read the poem by Emily Dickinson out loud and then silently.
- List the denotative and connotative meanings of words in the chart below. You can use an online or print dictionary.

WORD	DENOTATIVE MEANING	CONNOTATIONS
clover		
bee		
revery		
few		

- In the space below, discuss the meaning of the poem using the denotative and connotative meanings of the four words in the chart.

_____
_____
_____
_____
_____

Reprinted from *Vocabulary Is Comprehension* by Laura Robb. Thousand Oaks, CA: Corwin. Reproduction authorized only for the local school site or nonprofit organization that has purchased this book.

Goals: In this lesson, students review denotative meanings and find connotative or associated meanings for each word. You select two to three words from the list that students created during a 5-day study of a root(s). In this sample lesson, I use words related to the roots *viv* and *vit*. The aim is for students to develop connotative meanings of the words, thereby deepening their understanding of the words. They also come to appreciate that when they read, part of their responsibility is indeed to intuit and reflect on connotations. Authors consciously or unconsciously choose words that carry important associations—connotations that affect theme, inferences, characters' traits, decisions, settings, and so on.

Word(s)	Definition
revitalize	to mend, to breathe new life into
revive, revived, reviving	to bring to life again
reviver	a person who brings someone back to life again
survive, survived, surviving	to be able to live and stay alive
survivor	a person who makes it through a tough experience
vital	needed for living
vitals	body signs such as heartbeat and blood pressure that show health
vitamin	a pill that makes you healthy
vivacious	full of life and energy
vivisection	operations on living animals to study their organs and diseases
vivid	brightly colored, lively

Definitions students suggested for words relating to *viv* and *vit*.

Materials: Two to three words from a weekly root and affix lesson, chart paper or a computer and whiteboard, copies of the reproducible Denotative and Connotative Meanings of Words (see **www.corwin.com/vocabularyiscomprehension**)

This lesson uses *survive, survived, surviving, survival,* and *vital, vitality* from the lesson on the roots *viv, vit* on page 126.

▶ Organize students into small groups of three to five students.

▶ Have groups choose a recorder, a person who jots down members' ideas.

▶ Return to the chart on page 126 and review the denotative meanings of survival and vital.

▶ Ask groups to discuss connotations or associations of each word.

▶ Create a chart with the word, its denotative meaning, and connotations.

Word and Multiple Forms	Denotative Meaning	Connotations
survive, survived, surviving survival, survivor	to be able to stay alive	trauma such as an accident, emotional, school, a person who remains alive after someone close dies, withstand extreme weather and/or situations, proper economically, germs and bacteria, scandals, religious practices, family traditions
vital, vitality	vital: needed for living vitality: high energy, strong	statistics, the U.S. census, medication, exercise, helmet, leadership, organs, vitamins, water, role in a play or organization, breathing capacity

Denotative and connotative meanings suggested by a sixth-grade class.

▶ Have students sit in the same groups.

▶ Invite groups to discuss how knowing connotations can improve their understanding of narratives, informational texts, and poetry. Tell groups that they can find an example from their instructional and/or independent reading.

▶ Ask groups to share and discuss their findings with one another.

▶ Have students sit in the same groups.

▶ Give each group two words from one of your lessons on prefixes, suffixes, and roots.

▶ Ask groups to write a denotative meaning for each word.

▶ Invite students to gather connotations.

▶ Organize a chart into three columns or create columns on your computer:

Word   Denotative Meanings   Connotations

▶ Have groups share their findings and write them on chart paper or project onto a whiteboard.

Day 4

▶ Have students complete the reproducible.

Tips for English Language Learners and Developing Readers

▶ Include students reading several years below grade level in different groups so students can hear and observe classmates' thinking. Understand that they will not absorb all the information, but these students can start building a mental model of denotative and connotative meanings.

▶ Support newcomers and ELL students who lack facility with English by helping them understand the word's denotative meanings and using words in oral sentences and conversation.

▶ Have middle grade and middle school ELL students who have solid English skills work with a group.

▶ Circulate and support groups' process and students who require your help by asking questions that engage students in talking about the diverse situations in which a word can be used.

Game On!

Word games can provide extra practice for students at diverse reading levels. Explore online games by using Google and invite students to play games at school during independent work times. You can focus your Google search for games for prefixes and suffixes or for roots or synonyms and antonyms. Or you can invite students to create vocabulary games to share with their classmates.

You'll find lots of vocabulary-building games and meaningful word work at *Divide, Conquer, Combine, and Create: A Vocabulary Learning Routine for Grades 3–8* by Tim Rasinski, Nancy Padak, Rick Newton, and Evangeline Newton (2007); go to http://www.timrasinski.com/presentations/IRA07Tim_Rasinski.pdf

What's sure to happen is that students will play these word games at home and strengthen their knowledge of prefixes, suffixes, and Greek and Latin roots.

Collaborate and Learn

Discuss these prompts and questions with a colleague or at a team or faculty meeting.

1. Bring sample lessons on roots and affixes to the group and discuss what worked, what you want to improve, and how this knowledge supports students' vocabulary development.

2. Why is it important to understand situations in which a word works?

3. How can consistent instruction meet the Common Core vocabulary standards and at the same time improve students' comprehension of complex texts?

4. Play some online vocabulary games with a colleague or group during planning time or a faculty meeting. By familiarizing yourself with each game, you can make recommendations to students and support their needs.

CHAPTER 5

General Academic and Domain-Specific Vocabulary

Last fall, a fifth-grade teacher asked me to observe his class and coach him on his vocabulary instruction. When I arrived, students were in the midst of copying key words and their definitions from the chalkboard before reading about simple machines: *lever, fulcrum, effort, load, inclined plane, first- and second-class levers, mechanical advantage, resistance*. When they were finished, the teacher reviewed the words and their meanings and asked students to open their textbooks and read the first three pages of the chapter on simple machines. The teacher and I moved around the room, watching for students who needed support.

A few minutes later, I heard a textbook slam shut at a nearby desk. A boy named Jake sat there with an "I'm so done," expression on his face. "Can I help?' I asked.

"Sure you can—give me the words so I can read this stuff!" he said, with frustration, even despair, in his voice. I pulled up a chair and looked at the vocabulary load on the three assigned textbook pages. I asked Jake to try reading the pages again and point to the words that were tripping him up. In addition to the domain- or content-specific words his teacher had briefly covered, there were several general academic words like *structure*, *location*, and *circumstances* that eluded Jake.

There are thousands of students like Jake in classrooms around the United States. Bright, capable students who want to learn but are made to feel inadequate by an unfortunate combination of weak reading ability and highly challenging texts across disciplines. These students lack the general academic vocabulary to read and comprehend grade-level, complex materials. I would argue that having to strictly adhere to pacing guides and teaching to high-stakes tests has added to their struggles. If we respond to these students' needs, we can help them.

Research has shown time and again that students who have a large general academic vocabulary read complex texts well and that general academic vocabulary knowledge is the strongest indicator of success at school (Dunn, Bonner, & Huske, 2007; Graves, 2008). Without lessons and interventions that expand students' general academic vocabulary, students like Jake will be unprepared to cope with sophisticated, complex texts in middle and high school (Dunn et al., 2007; Hiebert, 2013; Hiebert & Lubliner, 2008; Kelley, Lesaux, Kieffer, & Faller, 2010; Marzano, 2004, 2009a; Marzano & Pickering, 2005; Park, 2013–2014).

In this chapter, we look head-on at how to teach in ways that help students like Jake as well as proficient readers. You'll see that teaching general academic and domain-specific vocabulary is intertwined with teaching reading and engaging with texts across disciplines. Why? Because these are the words found in content areas and to know them is often to know complex, sometimes abstract concepts, which is the challenge learners face.

Let's look at the College and Career Readiness Anchor Standards for Reading as a way of seeing how the specialized vocabulary of learning grafts onto what we expect students to be able to do as readers. These anchor standards, which define the reading skills that students in K–12 must demonstrate, incorporate many of what Hiebert and Lubliner (2008) classify as "school-task words." These are general academic words that students need for specific tasks as readers, like analyzing texts; students also meet these words on school tests, state tests, and in directions for reading and writing tasks.

The CCR Anchor Standards for Reading

Standard 1: Read closely to determine what the text says explicitly and to make logical inferences from it; cite specific textual evidence when writing or speaking to support conclusions drawn from the text.

Standard 2: Determine central ideas or themes of a text and analyze their development; summarize the key supporting details and ideas.

Standard 3: Analyze how and why individuals, events, and ideas develop and interact over the course of a text.

Standard 4: Interpret words and phrases as they are used in a text, including determining technical, connotative, and figurative meanings, and analyze how specific word choices shape meaning or tone.

Standard 5: Analyze the structure of texts, including how specific sentences, paragraphs, and larger portions of the text (e.g., a section, chapter, scene, or stanza) relate to each other and the whole.

Standard 6: Assess how point of view or purpose shapes the content and style of a text.

Standard 7: Integrate and evaluate content presented in diverse media and formats, including visually and quantitatively, as well as in words.

Standard 8: Delineate and evaluate the argument and specific claims in a text, including the validity of the reasoning as well as the relevance and sufficiency of the evidence.

Standard 9: Analyze how two or more texts address similar themes or topics in order to build knowledge or to compare the approaches the authors take.

Standard 10: Read and comprehend complex literary and informational texts independently and proficiently.

Quick Recap: How the Lessons in This Book Address the Anchor Standards

The recurring theme of this book is this: Vocabulary *is* comprehension. We can't read and learn if we don't know the words. I know that sounds so patently obvious, but I say it here to underscore that each chapter of this book is meant to bridge the divide between vocabulary instruction and reading instruction. The lessons in Chapters 2 and 3 teach vocabulary with a short complex text or poem so that students get that immediate practice of applying word knowledge in "new" authentic reading situations. In the course of the 5 days of partner work and class discussion, students practice anchor standard skills such as

▶ Retell

▶ Infer

▶ Find theme

▶ Read closely

▶ Use text details and connotative meanings of words to support interpretations

▶ Write to explain themes, inferences, main ideas

Chapter 4's lessons on word parts and roots require students to connect words to themes and topics and read their instructional and independent texts with an eye to interpreting words and phrases and considering how their meanings related to words they knew with the same roots. Now, here in Chapter 5, the lessons invite students to practice with texts they're reading in different disciplines. Here and as always, I recommend that when you select words to teach, cull them from materials students are reading so that you'll naturally build content area comprehension too.

Forging connections between building vocabulary and students' reading is crucial, for it raises students' awareness of how words can make or break their understanding of—and engagement with—texts. Refer to the anchor reading standards as one resource when planning vocabulary lessons or developing student assignments that deal with school tasks and deliberately use words from them—*explain, cite, contrast, develop*; make sure students fully comprehend what these words ask of them. Do the same with reading lessons, having students analyze texts using these same general academic terms. You'll find more detailed lists of general academic words to use as a resource for culling words from texts students read on the Corwin website (see **www .corwin.com/vocabularyiscomprehension**).

Four Categories of Academic Vocabulary

Hiebert and Lubliner (2008) divide academic vocabulary into four vocabulary groups:

▶ General academic

▶ Content-specific

▶ School-task

▶ Literary

Hiebert and Lubliner categorized in this way as a means of examining the frequency with which words in any given category appear in texts. By slicing and dicing in this way, teachers can have a means of prioritizing which words to teach, how to teach them, and for how long. All four categories are important, for sure, but hands down, general academic vocabulary is most critical to focus lessons on. Not only do general academic words appear more frequently in texts than do words from the other categories, but these words also appear across disciplines that students study (Hiebert & Lubliner, 2008).

The Categories Defined

Content-Specific Vocabulary. Found in math, science, and social studies. These words are specific to a topic within a subject and appear in texts written about a specific subject. In math, examples are *fractions, proper fractions, improper fractions, decimals*; in science, examples are *plant cell, cell wall, cellulose, cell division*; and in social studies, examples are *pharaoh, pyramid, afterlife, canopic jars, papyrus scrolls*.

School-Task Vocabulary. These are words used in directions for tests and quizzes, for the writing process, and to assess reading comprehension. Examples include *analyze, explain, argue for, define, summarize, draft, revise, edit*. It's important to teach school-task words to all students to provide them with a thorough knowledge of each word's meaning because task words are part of directions students must comprehend at school and on state-mandated tests. By including school-task words in the anchor text reading standards, the Common Core highlights the importance of this type of vocabulary. A deep knowledge of school-task words enables students to close read complex texts in order to explore layers of meaning, as well as unpack the intent of directions, and apply them to a task.

Literary Vocabulary. Words that describe characters and their thoughts and actions, settings, conflicts, and problems are words found in literature. Hiebert and Lubliner point out that literary words might not appear often in conversation and in texts, giving them a low-frequency rating. Moreover, the authors point out that writers of literature will use different words to describe the same concept. For example, words that describe the concept of fear can be *terrified, panic, agitation, distress, dread*, and the like. Though the words relate to fear, each word connotes different associations and situations. The literary writer chooses words based on a story's context and the feelings he or she hopes to convey.

General Academic Vocabulary. These words support students' reading of texts in multiple disciplines. They should be taught across disciplines because they are an integral part of literary, informational, and content-specific reading material. Words such as *acquire, alternative, appropriate, circumstance, comment, conditions features, fund, finance, independent, imply, institute, indicate, highlight, scheme, specific, statement, sufficient*, and so on are part of general academic vocabulary; their meanings frequently change in different content area subjects. For example, the meaning of *equality* in civics differs from the meaning of *equality* in social studies. Likewise, the meaning of *document* in social studies can be a written law such as the constitution, whereas in English, it means to provide evidence or a bibliography. And in math, a *rational* number is a real number that can be written as a fraction, but a *rational* argument in a text is an argument that makes sense because it is based on logic and information. Context and discipline can change the meaning of the same word. In our language, the same word can have multiple meanings, making vocabulary study complex for all readers and challenging for ELL students and developing readers.

The Best Use of Word Lists

Word lists abound in books, online, and in our own school curricula. They can be seductive. They have this inherent authoritativeness, and even after decades in the classroom, I can come across one that makes me think, "Wow, this is the missing piece that will help my underperforming students." But at the end of the day, they are just lists of words and not words connected to content and experiences that students are engaging with. You might find it helpful to revisit the section "Which Words Do I Teach?" on pages 16–17 in Chapter 2.

That said, I have included some word lists (see **www.corwin.com/vocabulary iscomprehension**) that I think are good. One is by Dr. Averil Coxhead (2000), Victoria University, Wellington, and contains the word and its frequency found in texts. Another is a list of academic words compiled by Jim Burke and grade-level lists for fourth through eighth grades created for the Word Up Project (https://www.flocabulary.com/vocabulary-lessons/). By sifting through these lists, you can see the wide range of academic words that proficient and advanced readers have. The lists are a resource for you. The intention is not for you to teach every word on the lists, but to use the lists to select academic words that relate to your units, print and e-book reading materials, and videos. Always teach the words in an authentic context so students can experience how a word works in diverse situations.

Ideally, vocabulary instruction is planned in a schoolwide initiative or at the very least, with grade-level teams who can look at various word lists together and consider them in light of the curriculum. This same recommendation applies to the next section, which addresses the considerations about the particular students in your school and the particulars of your curriculum across the content areas.

Have students complete the reproducible Rate Your Own Word Knowledge in order to get a better sense of what your students already know.

Narrowing the List

A second important factor in deciding which words to teach is to discover what your students already know so that you can immediately rule out words most students have a solid understanding of—words they can readily use to think, speak, and write. An excellent strategy for determining word strength is to use the reproducible Rate Your Word Knowledge (see lesson on pages 140–143 of this chapter and **www.corwin.com/vocabularyiscomprehension**). By inviting students to rate their word knowledge, you can determine which words the entire class and/or groups need to learn. It's a good place to start with students who are reading in the bottom quartile as well as with English language learners (ELLs) because it helps you see what students know and which words you need to teach. The issue that teachers wrestle with is knowing which words to choose from diverse reading materials.

A third important factor in selecting words is to consider words that will give you the biggest bang for the buck across disciplines. In this light, school-task words and general academic vocabulary are a must. School-task words are part of students' school life starting in kindergarten; a deep understanding of these words can support success in completing tasks at school and in the workplace.

School-Task Words

It's beneficial if teachers across disciplines and grades meet to discuss the school-task words that students use at their grade level and create grade-level lists of these words that they revisit and adjust annually. For example, first-grade teacher, Hanna Robinson, at Quarles Elementary school in Winchester, Virginia, frequently uses these words in all subjects: *draw, draw and write, explain, sort, categorize, compare, sequence, heading, infer, notice, predict, purpose, support, show, setting, character, pattern, quotation,* and *restate.*

The list of school-task words is larger in the fifth grade class at the same school. This list includes all of the first-grade words plus the following: *abbreviate, analyze, argue, assess, audience, brainstorm, caption, characteristic, complete, conclude, defend, diminish, draft, edit, equal, equivalent, essay, essential, evaluate, evidence, example, identify, include, inquiry, italics, main, metaphor, narrative, narrator, opinion, paraphrase, persuade, point of view, preview, procedure, proofread, quote, relationship, review, revise, scan, significance, simile, skim, structure, sum, summarize, summary, support, theme, timeline, topic, trait, voice.*

Most teachers don't consciously cull these words and teach the word(s) as students need them. We assume that after elementary school, students know these words. However, many don't know them well enough to successfully apply them to complex tasks such as writing an essay, reading a grade-level complex text, or answering text-specific questions.

Suggestions for Teaching School-Task Words

On the First Day

- Teach the word when students will need and use it.
- Think aloud to show how you use the word. This builds students' mental model of how the word works with a specific task.
- Ask students to turn to a partner and talk about what they know about the word.
- Collect on chart paper or project onto a whiteboard what students know.

After Students Use the Word

- Invite students to add to the list of what they know about the word after applying the word to a task.

- Review what students understand when they need the word for a specific task.

- Gather students who require additional practice and start by asking them what they recall and understand about the word. Knowing what students know will enable you to decide whether you need to return to thinking aloud or whether to ask students to discuss the word and how it helps them complete a specific task.

Why General Academic Vocabulary Is Key

Beck, McKeown, and Kucan refer to general academic vocabulary as "high-utility words" (2002, 2013). These words are high utility because students bump into them frequently in reading materials across disciplines. Michael Graves (2008) points out that students' reading vocabulary grows at about 3,000 to 4,000 words a year while they're in school. By eighth grade, students have a reading vocabulary of 25,000 words, and by the end of high school, 50,000 words.

For this vocabulary growth to take place, students need to have a rich and varied independent reading life in addition to reading for diverse disciplines at school. It's those 40 to 60 extra books read annually that can accelerate vocabulary development and reading achievement (Allington, 2009; Kittle, 2013; Krashen, 1993; Miller, 2009; Robb, 2010, 2013).

However, some children enter school with a small oral vocabulary, and this can be a serious deterrent to success in reading in school (Biemiller, 1999, 2004; Chall & Jacobs, 2003; Hart & Risley, 2003a). English language learners, when they enter school in the United States, come with a limited oral and reading English vocabulary. To close the reading gap for ELLs and developing readers, the focus of vocabulary lessons should be on general academic vocabulary because knowing these words will support students' reading and thinking in all disciplines (Maxwell, 2013).

Why Not Focus on Content-Specific Words?

According to Hiebert and Lubliner (2008), the frequency of general academic words is the number of times a word can be found in 1 million words of a text. The frequency rate for social studies words is 9.7 as compared to 71.7 for general academic words (p. 109). Moreover, content-specific words are usually well defined in a text by definition and/or a labeled graphic that clearly explains a process such as mitosis or the three branches of government.

The choice is clear—focus on directly teaching general academic words that are in the texts and materials students read. This doesn't mean that I recommend that you never teach content-specific words. Always teach words with poor context clues and those that are crucial to thinking about a specific topic.

Basic Elements of General Academic Vocabulary Lessons

You'll find a combination of these elements in the vocabulary lessons for The Big 10 (see Chapter 2, pages 10–13) and in the lessons on pages 140–154 in this chapter: meaningful discussions, teachers' demonstrations and think-alouds, writing, studying sample sentences, and making connections between and among words. Offering opportunities for rich, shared discussions is key to word learning; listening to spoken language starts at birth, some would say *in utero*, and remains throughout life an important method for expanding vocabulary.

Sample Lesson: Teaching the Word *Combine*

Keep your lessons to 10 to 15 minutes a day which means that you will need 2 to 3 days to complete a cycle.

Introduce one word and the meanings of the word. Following is the lesson based on the word *combine*.

1. Say the word, explain what you know about the word, and compose sentences that show how the meanings you discussed work.

For *combine* I say:

This is an interesting word because if the accent changes from the first to the second syllable, the meaning and part of speech changes. The noun combine (accent on first syllable) is a farm machine that harvests grains and crops or a group of people who work together. The verb combine (accent on the second syllable) means to join or merge.

Next, I write three sample sentences on the chalkboard that demonstrate how each word can work.

▶ The farmer rode his <u>combine</u> up and down his cornfield as the machine cut the corn, removed its kernels, and pushed the kernels into a large hopper.

▶ The state charged that cable companies formed an illegal <u>combine</u> to control consumer costs.

▶ American Airlines and US Airways <u>combined</u> their companies to form one large airline.

2. Ask students to turn to a partner and discuss everything they know about the word: its meanings, other forms, where they have seen or heard the word. Invite pairs to share what they know and create a list on chart paper or project the list onto a whiteboard.

Here are the forms of the word students offered: "combine, combined, combining, combination."

Students knew that combine *means to join or merge. They had used the word in math—to* combine *parts of an equation; some said for cooking—*combining *ingredients; all knew that corporations, like the airlines,* combined *to create one large company.*

}

3. Organize students into small groups and have them discuss everything they've learned about the word. Invite them to also discuss whether the word's meaning changes for different subjects they study at school.

Once you have introduced a word, like *combine*, ask students to partner up and make a list of everything they know about that word.

{ *Here's what students' shared:* combine *in math can refer to adding or multiplying numerals and fractions; in science, it can refer to putting two elements together such as oxygen and hydrogen to create water; in literature, it can refer to bringing two groups together; in sports,* combine *can mean joining junior and senior varsity teams; and in social studies, it can mean joining two separate laws or congressional committees.*

4. Help students explore and list situations the word can be used in—include situations for multiple meanings of the word.

{ *Here are the situations students offered for* combine, *meaning to merge or join.*

- ◗ Cooking
- ◗ Chemistry class or laboratory
- ◗ Planting
- ◗ Doctor's treatment
- ◗ Government's departments
- ◗ Sports teams
- ◗ Story elements: settings, character traits
- ◗ Laws
- ◗ Gangs, cliques, clubs, organizations
- ◗ Elements

◗ Cells

◗ Blood plasma

5. Have partners use their knowledge of situations to craft sentences for the word and its multiple meanings and forms. Share these with the class so students observe a range of possibilities.

Here is a sampling of students' sentences.

◗ In September, the gardener <u>combined</u> potting soil and peat moss before planting spring bulbs.

◗ A <u>combination</u> of fresh strawberries, vanilla ice cream, whipped cream, and sponge cake helped create this tasty strawberry shortcake.

◗ The coach is thinking of <u>combining</u> varsity and junior varsity soccer teams for the district playoffs.

◗ By <u>combining</u> a strong antibiotic and multivitamins, the vet brought the puppy back to health.

The five steps on pages 137–139 can deepen students' understanding of the general academic vocabulary that you explicitly teach. I've also included on pages 140–154 in this chapter some familiar, classroom-tested lessons that are extremely effective for expanding students' word knowledge.

Lessons for Teaching General Academic Words

In the next section, I share six lessons that have just the right amount of challenge, according to students with whom I work.

Rate Your Word Knowledge

Complex Text:

1866 Public Resolution

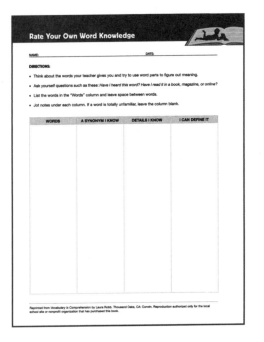

This 1866 Public Resolution is transcribed from the Thirty-ninth Congress, Sess. I, Res. 11. Statutes at Large, Treaties, and Proclamations, of the United States of America, Vol. XIV, George P. Sanger, ed. (Boston: Little, Brown, 1868).

A Resolution providing for Expenses incurred in searching for missing Soldiers of the Army of the United States, and for the further Prosecution of the same.

WHEREAS Miss Clara Barton has, during the late war of the <u>rebellion</u>, expended from her own <u>resources</u> large sums of money in endeavoring to discover missing soldiers of the armies of the United States, and in <u>communicating</u> intelligence to their relatives; Therefore—

Resolved by the Senate and House of Representatives of the United States of America in Congress <u>assembled,</u> That the sum of fifteen thousand dollars be, and the same is hereby, <u>appropriated,</u> out of any moneys in the Treasury not otherwise appropriated, to reimburse Miss Clara Barton for the amount so expended by her, and to aid in the further prosecution of the search for missing soldiers; and the printing necessary in the furtherance of the said object shall hereafter be done by the public printer. APPROVED, March 10, 1866.

Goals: This lesson is ideal for informing you before students read a particular text which words they understand and which words they know nothing about. Select four to eight general academic words or a key word in the text that has no context clues words for students to rate. The list can become students' purpose for reading: learning the meanings of the words and how the words connect to information in the text. The list can also become your vocabulary lessons for a group or the entire class when the lesson shows that students have no knowledge of the words.

I recommend that you do not grade this activity so that students feel comfortable about figuring out what they do and don't know. After you explicitly teach the words and students have read the text for the gist, have them return to the chart on the reproducible Rate Your own Word Knowledge and add what they've learned about each word.

I have adjusted the form by removing the last column, "This Word Is Unfamiliar to Me." Teachers have told me that students go right to this column instead of rummaging their minds to find some details and connections to a word.

Materials: Copies of the reproducible Rate Your Own Word Knowledge (see **www.corwin.com/vocabularyiscomprehension**); words chosen from the text selection: *rebellion, resources, communicating, assembled, appropriated* (these words also happen to appear on Dr. Coxhead's list, which is also on the Corwin site); use the text that goes with this lesson, or choose your own text

---

Day 1

▶ Give each student a copy of the Rate Your Word Knowledge reproducible.

▶ Write the five words on the chalkboard: *rebellion, resources, communicating, appropriated, assembled.*

▶ Have students copy the words into the first column of the form, leaving enough space between words for notes.

▶ Say each word so students hear the correct pronunciation.

▶ Invite students to try to recall where and when they heard or read the word. Ask them to think of prefixes and roots they might know.

▶ Ask students to work alone and think about what they know about the word.

- Have students jot notes under any or all of the other three columns on their form.

- Tell students that it's okay if they don't know any of the words. This will inform your decision to teach or not to teach the words.

- Collect students' work.

Day 2

- Review students' work for Rate Your Word Knowledge form.

- Make a decision based on what students know about the words: (1) Explicitly teach the words; (2) have students use discovering more about the words as their purpose for reading; (3) support a group who needs more instruction and have the rest of the class read the text.

- Discuss the selection focusing on the meanings of the five words and how the words relate to the meaning of the text.

Tips for English Language Learners and Developing Readers

- Read the selection out loud and then ask students to read it.

- Work with this group and give them examples for each word. For example, for *assembly*, you can mention that the class goes to an assembly every week. Or you can use the word in a sentence and write it on a whiteboard and have the group use context to figure out its meaning.

- Reduce the number of words students work on if you feel fewer words will result in greater success.

- Return to the words several times and have students discuss what they remember about each one.

How I Might Follow This Lesson

- Return students' original Rate Your Word Knowledge Form.

- Have students underline the notes they took prior to the study.

- Ask students to add details to their Rate Your Word Knowledge form and share what they've learned with a classmate.

- Support any students who still lack an understanding of some words:

  ○ Write sentences with strong context clues that illustrate a word's meaning.

  ○ Have students use an online dictionary to deepen their understanding of specific words.

  ○ Encourage students to link the word to the topic and point out information that can help them remember the word's meaning.

Seventh grader Natalee underlines what she knows before studying the words with her teacher. After she studies the words in context, Natalee will add more information.

Rate Your Own Word Knowledge

NAME: Natalee Grubbs   DATE:

DIRECTIONS:

- Think about the words your teacher gives you and try to use word parts to figure out meaning.

- Ask yourself questions such as these: *Have I heard this word? Have I read it in a book, magazine, or online?*

- List the words in the "Words" column and leave space between words.

- Jot notes under each column. If a word is totally unfamiliar, leave the column blank.

WORDS	A SYNONYM I KNOW	DETAILS I KNOW	I CAN DEFINE IT
Barrage	a lot / tons many	adjective	a ton/lots
Devestating	tradgic	adjective	really bad or tradgic
Pensively	Carefully thoughtfully	adjective	thoughtfully
torrent	strong and fast-moving stream of water	noun	~~noun~~ fast moving stream of water
Perpetual	Constant	adject	constant
Unbridled	uncontrolled	adjective	uncontrolled
dispel	resolve	verb	get rid of resolve
bedlum	chaos	verb	~~become flimsy~~ Confusion
~~Clarity~~ Flail	Flimsy/rise	adjective	become flimsy
Clarity	To be clear	noun	quality of being clear

ABC List and Link

Goals: An adaptation of "ABC Brainstorm" (www.readingquest. org), this strategy can help you determine whether students have the background knowledge to begin a unit of study because students must do two things:

1. List as many words as they can think of that relate to the unit's topic for each letter of the alphabet

2. Connect the words to the topic

To show students their progress at the end of the study, have them complete a second ABC List and Link reproducible. Students can compare their prereading and postreading work on the ABC List and Link form and discuss the progress they have made with a partner or in a small group.

Words on the list will be a mix of general academic and domain-specific words. If students' prereading work shows that they know few to no words, then it's important to build their prior knowledge of the topic through videos, photographs, and teacher read-alouds.

Materials: Topic of your unit of study, copies of the reproducible ABC List and Link (see **www.corwin.com/vocabularyiscomprehension**)

Day 1

▶ Tell students the topic of the unit of study. The topic my students will study is slavery.

▶ Organize students into groups of four.

▶ Have groups discuss everything they know about slavery past and present.

▶ Give each student a copy of the reproducible ABC List and Link and review the directions. I give students 5 to 10 minutes to complete the form and explain that it's okay to skip round the alphabet and fill in words for any letters. Circulate and observe students at work to decide whether to end the activity early or give students more time.

▶ Collect students' work and read their responses to decide whether you can start the study or need to build students' prior knowledge by showing them video clips or photographs and/or reading aloud.

Tips for English Language Learners and Developing Readers

▶ Refer to the photos, videos, and read-alouds you did to help students generate vocabulary related to the unit. You might have to reread some selections and have students view videos and photos again.

- Helps students understand that the words they know that relate to slavery are the background knowledge they need to read and comprehend.

- Discuss connections to the topic with this group before they try to write them on the form.

How I Might Follow This Lesson

- At the end of the study, ask students to complete, on their own, a second ABC List and Link form in 5 to 10 minutes. Extend the time if students show you they need it.

- Invite students to discuss, with a partner, the progress that occurred by having them compare their first ABC sheet with the second.

- Have partners share the words on their second list with the entire class so everyone can expand his or her vocabulary.

Concept Map and Writing

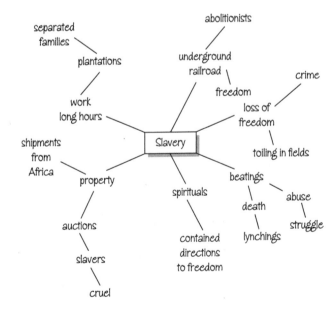

Goals: This is a whole-class word and concept-building activity that should be revisited two to three times a week during a unit of study. You'll need a theme or concept that relates to your unit of study, such as *devastation, conformity, justice/injustice, friendship, slavery,* and so on. Start the concept map before students receive reading materials so that their suggestions cover a wide range of associations. Once students read materials, the information narrows their focus and choices.

Since this is a whole-class activity, ELL students and developing readers have multiple opportunities to hear the responses of classmates and build their knowledge of the concept or theme and related words. Words and phrases that students suggest will be a mix of general academic and domain-specific vocabulary.

Materials: A concept or theme that relates to a unit of study, copies of the reproducible Concept Map and Writing, chart paper and marker pens or a whiteboard and computer

---

Day 1

▶ Prepare the chart or whiteboard by writing the concept in the center of the paper. Place students' suggestions around the concept (see sample), which is on slavery.

Response Reminders
Create a class list of students' names. Each time a student responds, place the date next to her name. The list is your reminder of who has answered so you can call on volunteers who have not yet responded.

▶ Introduce the theme or concept before plunging into the unit. I introduce *friendship* and write it on chart paper.

▶ Spend no more than 3 to 5 minutes collecting students' ideas. Explain the time limits and tell students that each time you return to this activity you'll call on different students.

❱ Model how you suggest a detail or idea that relates to friendship, and then connect your idea to the concept. Here's what I say:

> Common interests like playing hoops and soccer can develop a friendship. The connection I'm making is that if two people enjoy the same things, it can be their reason for becoming friends. Notice what I did. I stated my reason for friendships—common interests—and then I linked my statement to friendship. When you answer, give a specific example and link it to why the example can support friendship.

❱ Organize students into partners.

❱ Invite pairs to talk and decide on one detail, a phrase, or a snippet of a story that relates to the concept of friendship. Remind partners to connect their idea to the concept of friendship.

Here are two suggestions from fifth graders:

Loyal—a friend is loyal and stands up for you when you're in trouble.

Moving—when a friend moves far away, you want to stay in touch, but it [the friendship] fizzles out over time.

❱ Write students' suggestions on the chart.

❱ Review ideas on the chart each time you return to it, and then invite students to add details to the notes on the chart or suggest different ideas.

❱ Have students complete the reproducible.

Day 2

Online Word Games

Marzano (2004, 2005) recommends that students play word games to deepen their knowledge of general academic vocabulary. Besides being interactive, and just plain fun, words games support memory, critical thinking, and spelling and can help develop students' social skills.

Students can play board games such as *Scrabble* (Milton Bradley) and *Boggle* (Parker Brothers) during class, and they also enjoy playing online word games. By Googling "online vocabulary games" you'll find an abundance of websites to investigate and vocabulary games designed for specific grade levels and disciplines. Encourage your tech-savvy students to create original word games for classmates to play!

Words in the World

Words in the World

NAME: _____ DATE: _____

Write the word and its different forms here: _____

DIRECTIONS: Look for your word and its different forms over two to three days. Listen for it in conversations, videos, movies, blogs, while texting, in comics, billboards, signs, and magazines, online blogs, while shopping.

Word sightings: Where did you see and/or hear the word?

_____
_____

Explain how the word was used and what understandings about the word you learned from your sighting(s).

_____
_____
_____
_____
_____
_____
_____
_____
_____
_____
_____
_____

Goals: Words in the World is an outgrowth of In the Media by McKeown, Crosson, Artz, Sandora, and Beck (2013). This activity invites students to choose one or more words they've been learning and spot the words in the world. Instead of making the activity optional as McKeown et al. do, I require it of all students. Students can spot words on television, videos, the movies, comics, texting, online browsing, blogs, conversations, advertisements, magazines, newspapers, signs, directions, shopping, and so on. The goal is to show students that the words they learn at school are a vital part of life outside of school.

Materials: Copies of the reproducible Words in the World (see **www.corwin.com/vocabularyiscomprehension**), one word that each student chooses

Day 1

▶ Have students select a word they have studied. Guide the choice of ELL students and developing readers.

▶ Give students the Words in the World Form, and have them complete it in 2 to 4 days.

Day 2

Motivate and Engage Students
Using digital literacies such as wikis, blogs, and Twitter increases students' participation at school because teachers make learning relevant by tapping into students' digital worlds. The University of Minnesota works with high school English teachers to use Twitter and other social media in their classrooms because it raises students' engagement and achievement. Middle school teachers need to integrate 21st century literacies into all disciplines. You can watch this video by going to http://www.youtube.com/watch?v=4Oxlz_3o3O0&feature=related.

▶ Set aside 20 to 30 minutes of a class period and ask students to share their findings or place students' forms on a bulletin board and provide time for them to read one another's.

Tips for English Language Learners and Developing Readers

▶ Guide students' selection of a word to ensure that it's one they understand well.

▶ Have students complete the form after they find one word sighting. As students experience success, invite them to find extra sightings.

▶ Support students with writing about what they learned about the word by talking with individuals or pairs. Sighting words makes them relevant to life for students.

Fifth-grade student Lucas broadens his understanding of *hyperbole*.

Words in the World

NAME: Lucas   DATE:

Write the word and its different forms here: hallucination, halluceinate, hallucinated, hallucinating

DIRECTIONS: Look for your word and its different forms over two to three days. Listen for it in conversations, videos, movies, blogs, while texting, in comics, billboards, signs, and magazines, online blogs, while shopping.

Word sightings: Where did you see and/or hear the word?

in Flora and Ulysses By Kate Decamillo
my friends

Explain how the word was used and what understandings about the word you learned from your sighting(s).

My friends used it - Hallucination - seeing water on the desert. In the book Tootie accusess Flora that she's having a hallucinatio. - Ulysses is a super hero. It means seeing somthing thats not there - a fantasy thought.

Making Analogies on a Class Wiki or Blog

Goals: In this lesson, students analyze relationships between one pair of words in order to select a second pair with a similar relationship. In so doing, they are determining an analogy between the word sets, using their knowledge of meaning, form, and usage. The Common Core supports working with analogies because composing analogies requires that students figure out relationships between words and problem solve. If your students haven't worked with analogies, consider having them practice with analogies you can find online.

In this lesson format, groups of four students create original analogies challenges for classmates to complete using specific vocabulary and post them on a class wiki. Classmates then try to figure them out and suggest adjustments and alternative examples and choices to make the analogies stronger. If your students have a solid knowledge of analogies, you can skip to the third day's lesson on page 151.

Materials: Words that the class has studied: general academic, literary, domain specific; students select or the teacher assigns two to five words for each pair; copies of student handouts Types of Analogies and Create Original Analogies (see **www .corwin.com/vocabularyiscomprehension**)

Types of Analogies

Tips for Creating Analogies

- Choose the relationship between the first pair of words.
- Make sure the relationship is clear.
- Create four choices; one should clearly match the relationship between the first pair of words.
- Make two of the choices obviously incorrect.
- Make one of the choices almost correct.

  Example:
  Jupiter : solar system [the relationship is member of the category]
  Jupiter : solar system :: Milky Way : _____
  (a) candy bar; (b) galaxy; (c) stars; (d) distance

Synonyms
  surge : rise :: renew : restore

Antonyms
  vicious : kind :: reckless : careful

Rhyming Words
  thatch : catch :: loud : crowd

Whole/Part
  bakery : cookies :: environment : trees

Category/Subcategory
  primates : gorillas :: mollusks : snails

Homophones
  deer : dear :: capitol : capital

Cause/Effect
  rain : flooding :: heat : drought

Member/Category
  amoeba : protozoa :: trumpet : instrument

Object and Its Use
  knife : cutting :: money : saving

Reprinted from Vocabulary Is Comprehension by Laura Robb. Thousand Oaks, CA: Corwin. Reproduction authorized only for the local school site or nonprofit organization that has purchased this book.

Create Original Analogies

NAME: _____ DATE: _____

Words for analogies: _____

DIRECTIONS:

- Work with a partner.
- Create original analogies using words you have studied.
- Use the "Tips for Creating Analogies" on the "Types of Analogies" handout.
- Exchange papers with another pair of students and complete each other's analogies.
- Discuss your choices by joining both partnerships into a group of four.

_____
_____
_____
_____
_____
_____
_____
_____
_____
_____
_____
_____
_____
_____
_____
_____
_____

Reprinted from Vocabulary Is Comprehension by Laura Robb. Thousand Oaks, CA: Corwin. Reproduction authorized only for the local school site or nonprofit organization that has purchased this book.

Day 1

Introduce the format of analogies.

Materials: Sample analogy, whiteboard or chart paper and marker pens

▶ Use a whiteboard to project this analogy:

panic : terror :: reveal : disclose

▶ Explain how to read the analogy. The single colon stands for "is to;" the double colon, for "as." Read the analogy this way: panic is to terror as reveal is to disclose.

▶ Have students practice reading two to three other analogies.

▶ Invite students to try completing some analogies. You can Google "analogies" and "analogy games" and choose a site that's appropriate for your students.

Introduce different types of analogies with examples.

Day 2

Materials: Copies of student handout Types of Analogies (see **www.corwin.com/vocabularyiscomprehension**)

▶ Organize students into groups of four.

▶ Give each student a copy of the handout Types of Analogies.

▶ Have groups discuss the types of analogies and raise questions.

Day 3

▶ Help students understand that their goal is to figure out the relationship between the first pair of words so they can complete the second pair.

▶ Have students play analogy games that reinforce the different types. You'll find online games by Googling "analogy games."

Materials: Copies of the reproducible Create Original Analogies; specific words for creating analogies; computers, tablets, or iPads for students; class wiki

▶ Organize students into pairs.

▶ Give each pair two to three words. It's okay if pairs have the same words because their analogies will differ if you have them work on different types (see **www .corwin.com/vocabularyiscomprehension** for a list of types of analogies).

▶ Ask students to compose analogies that are not complete. Students leave the last part blank and offer four choices so classmates can choose one.

   Example: black : white :: war : _____

   a. guns   b. peace   c. soldiers   d. camouflage

▶ Have students post their original analogies on your class wiki.

▶ Ask students to try completing their classmates' analogies and suggest adjustments and different choices.

Tips for English Language Learners and Developing Readers

▶ Offer the challenge of creating original analogies to ELL students who have a command of English.

▶ Ask pairs to play online analogy games appropriate to their success level.

How I Might Follow Up the Lesson

▶ I might have students who have experience with analogies use the handout Types of Analogies to create original analogies using the reproducible Create Original Analogies (see **www.corwin.com/vocabularyiscomprehension**).

Twelve original analogies from groups of students in Grades 5 to 8: Students' original analogies illustrate high-level thinking and practice with using general and domain-specific words

1. daffodil : vase :: water : _____

   a. garden   b. pitcher   c. tea   d. mud

2. earth : sun :: electron : _____

   a. nucleus   b. oven   c. outlet   d. charge

3. blizzard : storm :: trumpet : _____

   a. man   b. taps   c. instrument   d. the army

4. scissors : cut :: pen : _____

   a. scribble   b. chew   c. ballpoint   d. write

5. ice : Eskimo :: desert : _____

   a. sand   b. nomads   c. heat   d. camels

6. white : purity :: red : _____

   a. roses   b. valentine   c. balloon   d. passion

7. poem : poet :: song : _____

   a. performer   b. band   c. composer   d. dancer

8. asteroid : rock :: comet : _____

   a. ice   b. gas   c. cleaner   d. iron

9. spider : arachnid :: whale : _____

   a. huge   b. fish   c. predator   d. mammal

10. hat : head :: monitor : _____

    a. computer   b. hearing aid   c. assess   d. DVD

11. time : watch :: north star : _____

    a. sky   b. direction   c. Milky Way   d. black hole

12. tiger : stripes :: giraffe : _____

    a. tall   b. orange   c. spots   d. leaves

Creating a Class Wiki

If you enter "how to create a class wiki" into an online search engine, you will find many choices for creating a class wiki.

Read about wikis and select the directions that work for you. You can ask a colleague who has a class wiki to help you get started. If your school has a tech-support person, ask him or her to get you started and keep you going!

Tweeting for Word Learning

Goals: Tweeting is ideal for word learning because students have to complete their analysis and show their thinking in 140 characters and spaces. The reproducible Tweeting to Show Understanding (see **www .corwin.com/vocabularyiscomprehension**) has headings that identify the type of tweet you might want students to complete and lines for writing the tweet; students can compose tweets on computers, tablets, or iPads, using the word count to check that characters and spaces don't exceed 140. Since tweeting uses the technology that students love, this activity is highly motivating.

Groups can have the same word but compose different tweets such as a word's connotations, a sentence with a synonym, and so on.

Students can tweet

- The word in a sentence

- Original analogies

- Words' connotative meanings

- Multiple meanings of the word

- Related words

- Synonyms or words with similar meanings

- A synonym in a sentence

- Antonyms or words with opposite meanings

- An antonym in a sentence

Materials: Copies of reproducible Tweeting to Show Understanding (see **www .corwin.com/vocabularyiscomprehension**)

- Review, if necessary, terms such as *synonym, antonym, connotations; related words; multiple forms and meanings; analogies*

Day 1

- Model how you complete several tweets. Here are some I model:

Sentence: Cows are domestic animals because they live on farms and not in the wild; they provide milk and beef for consumers.

A word, its forms and meanings: The word *just* has these forms: *justly, justice, unjust, justify*. It can mean fair or equitable, a short time ago, and only.

Synonyms and write one in a sentence: A synonym for *vex* is *infuriate*. "Not receiving an invitation to Cal's birthday party infuriated James who vowed never to talk to Cal again."

- Explain that tweets can be less than 140 characters, spaces, and punctuation, but not more.

Day 2

Day 3

▶ Give students a copy of the reproducible Tweeting to Show Understanding.

▶ Organize students into pairs and have partners compose two to three tweets.

▶ Pair-up partners with another pair and have this group of four share tweets with one another.

▶ Invite pairs to put their tweets on a class wiki or blog so their classmates can expand their word knowledge.

Tips for English Language Learners and Developing Readers

▶ Pair an ELL student or a developing reader with a proficient or advanced reader.

▶ Invite partners in this group to complete tweets that allow them to succeed: synonyms, antonyms, connotations; related words; multiple meanings of words.

▶ Provide support and guidance for those students who need it to experience success.

Students learn to be concise and know that it's tough to tweet if you don't understand a word.

ANTONYMS AND SYNONYMS

- Synonyms for *ecology* are *preservation, environmental protection,* and *conservation;* antonyms are *destruction, misuse,* and *extinction.*
- Synonyms for *complex* are *complicated, composite, compound, intricate, labyrinthine;* antonyms are *simple, unsophisticated, uncomplicated.*
- Antonyms for *dominant* are *subordinate, secondary, recessive* like a recessive trait, *prevalent* as frequently, like tornadoes in the Midwest.

SENTENCES TO SHOW UNDERSTANDING

- The Red Cross helps those in need by <u>distributing</u> food, blankets, medication, clothing, after twisters, blizzards, and hurricanes strike.
- The club <u>schemed</u> to be the top seller of boxes of candy by undercutting the price other organizations set for the same product.

MULTIPLE FORMS AND MEANINGS

- *Consume—consumed, consuming, consumer:* means engrossed as in a game, use up as in gas, destroy as in a fire, and devour, as beloved books.
- *Compensate—compensated, compensating, compensation, compensator, compensatory:* means to make up for a weakness, payment for services.

◆◆◆ Collaborate and Learn ◆◆◆

1. Discuss why it's crucial to build students' general academic vocabulary through discussions, writing, and playing online word games.

2. How can understanding school-task words support students' learning and work?

3. Why is it important to engage students in meaningful discussions about words?

4. Discuss ways you coach students who read below grade level to improve their comprehension by applying the Common Core anchor text reading standards to the vocabulary lessons and to materials they read.

Assessing Vocabulary

How do we best assess students' vocabulary development? It's helpful to first state *why* we are assessing what it is we are looking for. For me, it's a way to check progress so that I can adjust my instruction, so that in the course of the year my students gain the most ground they can in acquiring general academic and domain-specific vocabulary. For others, especially those who teach in schools that require a particular amount of grades per week, assessing in order to grade may be paramount in your mind. And if this is the case, you can use students' writing and their work on the reproducibles in this book for grading purposes.

The downside of grading is that it tends to make teachers focus too much on students' work product and keeps them from literally looking up and out to observe students in other moments of learning each day. I encourage you to reflect on your teaching and students' learning by observing students while they discuss and work in pairs and groups (Afflerbach, 2012; Greenstein, 2010; Tomlinson, 2007–2008). Also, read their written work with your teacher's eye and theory of learning in the forefront of your mind. Then shape-shift from assessing in order to grade to assessing in order to determine how each student received your lesson. What stuck? What didn't? Your thoughtful considerations will enable you to quickly support students who seem confused or "don't get it." Scaffold and intervene so students can build the foundation that enables them to complete challenging vocabulary tasks on their own and tackle, with confidence, texts they avoided because they lacked the skill and expertise to comprehend them.

So How Are They Reading Complex Texts?

Too often, spelling and vocabulary are taught as though they are these islands unto themselves, far away from the mainland of the curriculum. Beyond checking my students' vocabulary acquisition, I assess in order to evaluate how my vocabulary instruction has improved students' comprehension of complex, grade-level texts. After all, the purpose of extensive vocabulary instruction that addresses figurative language, word roots, denotative and connotative meanings, multiple forms and meanings of words, and so on is that all these things combine to help readers unlock meaning from complex texts.

Let's look at how a seventh grader would use a host of vocabulary tools to crack open a complex text. The following excerpt from Solomon Northup's memoir is one that could easily be used during a study of slavery and the Civil War. The movie *12 Years a Slave* made Northup's narrative popular, and it's now available as an e-book (http://docsouth.unc.edu/fpn/northup/northup.html). Northup's account of his life shows students a realistic picture of slaves' hardships and vile treatment at the hands of many masters. The narrative opens with Northup's birth and snapshots of his family. In this passage, Northup paints a portrait of his father:

Excerpt From *Twelve Years a Slave,* Narrative of Solomon Northup

Though born a slave, and laboring under the disadvantages to which my unfortunate race is subjected, my father was a man respected for his industry and integrity, as many now living, who well remember him, are ready to testify. His whole life was passed in the peaceful pursuits of agriculture, never seeking employment in those more menial positions, which seem to be especially allotted to the children of Africa. Besides giving us an education surpassing that ordinarily bestowed upon children in our condition, he acquired, by his diligence and economy, a sufficient property qualification to entitle him to the right of suffrage. He was accustomed to speak to us of his early life; and although at all times cherishing the warmest emotions of kindness, and even of affection towards the family, in whose house he had been a bondsman, he nevertheless comprehended the system of Slavery, and dwelt with sorrow on the degradation of his race. He endeavored to imbue our minds with sentiments of morality, and to teach us to place our trust and confidence in Him who regards the humblest as well as the highest of his creatures.

Not only is the vocabulary formidable for seventh-grade students, but the syntax—and the complexity of ideas embedded in long sentences—will challenge them. Thus, if students know more words going into a text like this and have experience determining meaning of unfamiliar terms or usage, they have a stronger chance of deriving meaning despite those long complex sentences. If, on the other hand, students struggle with vocabulary, the task of comprehending this text may be too frustrating and overwhelming.

Words are students' entrance ticket into complex texts and gaining admission to a literate, meaningful, and productive life. If we want our students to become skilled readers, writers, speakers, and thinkers, then the process begins and ends with word knowledge, because word knowledge is idea knowledge.

Informative Assessment and Responsive Teaching

How exactly do I assess complex text understanding, on top of daily lessons and all the other demands of the curriculum? To a large extent, I do it "on the fly"—that is, in the course of daily teaching and learning, I listen to students' talk about texts, their questions during vocabulary work, continually evaluating whether they are thinking about things with a sufficient level of understanding. I also look at their written work and maintain a certain mind-set: *What is this work showing me about the effectiveness of my teaching?*

So each and every day, I constantly assess: *Should I reteach with a new text? Should I scaffold part of the lesson? Should I pair this student with a classmate?*

This isn't hard once you do it, and in fact it is easier on you than waiting until some final test to discover your class hasn't understood weeks of teaching! The key here is to actively, quickly figure out what students understand and "get," to know what confuses and challenges them, and then to develop ways to scaffold or reteach if necessary. This is the essence of responsive teaching.

Carol Ann Tomlinson (2007–2008) uses the phrase "informative assessment," which I believe more accurately expresses the purpose of the known term, *formative assessment*. The purpose of collecting and studying informative assessments is to learn what students do well, to identify and understand specific needs, and to interpret these needs in order to develop interventions and scaffolds that enable students to improve. Continual progress for each student we teach is the primary goal of informative assessment. Progress occurs because informative assessments enable teachers to adjust their instructional moves and curriculum and respond to the needs students reveal each day (Afflerbach, 2012).

Here is an example of this responsive teaching in action. In Fay Stump's seventh-grade class, the lesson on personification went smoothly as long as students discussed the selection they read from "The Nightingale" (see Chapter 2, pages 26–30). It was completing the reproducible that challenged the English language learners and developing readers because they moved from analyzing reading to writing original texts that personified items. So I stepped in and retaught, scaffolding students by modeling my own process of first deciding how I wanted to personify a tornado—as vengeful or angry—and then thinking of a situation and using it to generate details. So I think out loud and say that I will have the vengeful tornado tear through a sleeping town, wreaking havoc and destruction; now I have the details to compose a sentence that personifies the tornado. Students then had a clear process to follow that enabled them to revise sentences, compose new ones, and successfully complete the written task.

Be Ready for Zigzags

Reteaching takes additional time, and so does giving students time to revise and complete their work. This is one of the biggest tensions in teaching—the pressure coming from above to cover a lot of curriculum and make a lot of progress and the pressure we put on ourselves to make sure our students are "getting it" on a day-to-day basis. To make sure we are on track day to day, we're going to have to accept that teaching and learning in general—and vocabulary lessons in particular—do not move steadily forward in a straight line. Instead, informative assessment results in back tracks, zigzags, and a disruption of the forward-moving flow of lesson plans and district pacing guides. But that's how teaching and learning work when our lessons respond to the needs students reveal.

You can become a highly successful assessor of daily vocabulary lessons by circulating, pausing at students' desks and tables, and offering support. The purpose of these minimeetings is to scaffold immediately or note the names of students who require more than a brief conversation (Sass-Henke, 2013). Always, the goal is to improve students' understanding and performance.

Why Final Tests Are Problematic

Unit tests, final exams, and high-stakes state tests are more about assigning grades and percentile rankings to measure what students have achieved, what they have learned. Moreover, mandated state tests, called summative assessments, usually occur in the spring when it's too late to use results to inform instruction because the school year is almost over.

Let's look at a concrete example of a student in an eighth-grade English class. At a state reading conference, Leah's teacher told me her student's story to vent her frustration with her district's unit tests and pacing guides. Leah (pseudonym) is on a sixth-grade instructional reading level. In Leah's middle school, like many middle schools in the United States, students take the same districtwide unit test and final exam. Leah earned a D on the districtwide English exam in November. Passing meant that she would go on to the next unit. However, Leah's deficits in making inferences, understanding the multiple meanings of words, developing a claim and arguing for it, explaining denotative and connotative meanings of specific words in a text were unchanged. There was no time to reteach or scaffold because the unit was over, and it was time to move on to biography.

Leah studied biography, but her deficits remained. As the year progressed, Leah's needs became obstacles to her learning and progress because improving students' performance throughout a unit did not occur. By the end of the year, Leah failed the final exam. When I heard Leah's story, the question that hit me was this: *Might she have passed and done much better if her teacher had provided intervention lessons and reteaching throughout the school year? Of course the answer is "yes."*

Compelling Research About Formative Assessment

One of the first studies on formative assessment offering evidence that this type of assessment worked was done in 1998 by two Englishmen: Paul Black and Dylan William. Both researchers completed a meta-analysis of more than 250 research studies on formative assessment. The pair concluded that formative assessment was the only way to raise standards in schools because it had a profound effect on students' learning.

Teaching students to self-assess became an important part of formative assessment (White & Frederiksen, 2000). Self-assessment can help students identify strengths and needs, and then students can set goals for improving. Students' goals that are an outgrowth of self-assessment become their "road map" for working hard to complete more challenging tasks and improve their conceptual understanding.

Dr. Robert J. Marzano's research on formative assessment in his book *Formative Assessment and Standards-Based Learning* (2009b) showed teachers how to use formative assessment to track students' progress; the type of assessment that Marzano believes is underutilized in today's classrooms is student-generated assessments. Such assessments permit students to decide how they will demonstrate their learning. For example, a student might show her understanding of personification by writing an original poem and leading a discussion of the poem with classmates; another student in the same class might decide to use a poem by Emily Dickinson to show his understanding of personification in a think aloud.

Gathering Data Throughout the Lessons

Even though the daily vocabulary lessons are brief, they yield rich information about students. Try to assess students' performance from the very start of each lesson so that you have the data to pace the lessons and ensure that every student is moving forward with word learning. To maintain the 10- to 15-minute time frame, I have suggested informative assessments that are brief and efficient and won't overwhelm you with data collecting (see pages 164–166).

You can use the Vocabulary Lesson Observation Form at **www.corwin.com/vocabularyiscomprehension** to quickly collect and interpret data each day you teach a vocabulary lesson. The Vocabulary Lesson Observation Form includes suggestions for observing students when introducing the lesson, what to notice about your students when they practice the skill, and what to tune into when you evaluate written work.

Making Instructional Decisions and Modifications

Once you consider and interpret data, you'll want to decide how you will support students' vocabulary learning. Decisions based on data collections can include the following:

▶ Preparing scaffolds for one student or a small group

▶ Reteaching the lesson the next day using a different and more accessible text

▶ Developing two or more short intervention lessons

▶ Pairing a student with a partner who has the expertise to help

▶ Presenting a second and similar lesson with different material for extra practice

▶ Designing process steps that scaffold students' learning

▶ Reserving extra time for the class or a group to complete written work

Finding extra time to help students is a challenge, but responding quickly can make a huge difference in their learning and performance. Here are suggestions for finding extra time:

▶ Add a few minutes to a vocabulary lesson the day you teach it.

▶ Use the 15-minute lesson time on one to three days to scaffold and support instead of introducing another vocabulary lesson.

▶ Meet with a group during lunch.

The list is my memory and reminders of who to help.

Vocabulary Lesson Observation Form

Vocabulary Lesson's Name: **Denotative + Connotative**

CLASS LIST	OBSERVATIONS: DAY 1ST, 2ND, 3RD	TEACHING MODIFICATIONS
Rosa	1st Finding connotation tough	Work with Rosa, Nate, Taria, + Josh. ① start w/ familiar words and practice orally
Juan		
Nate	2nd no connotative meanings	② Move to poem + discuss ③ Bring in another text/ poem to practice.
Jenna		
Taria	1st denotative fine no connotations	
Tony		
Richard		
Steven		
Lori		
Josh	2nd struggling w/ connotations	
Tanika		
Mara		
Caroline		
Hattie		
Emily		
Jamal		
Rodrigo		
Sallie		
Amber		

Clearing up confusions and providing extra instructional time—in other words, responding to what students "don't get"—means that students will be better equipped to deal with future lessons that incorporate similar skills and strategies and develop the vocabulary stamina to read and comprehend complex texts.

Introducing Lessons: The First Day

The first day of a lesson can let you know whether students can read the text. After I read a selection out loud, I always ask students to tell me words that are unfamiliar beyond the words selected for the lesson. If students don't know the meaning of too many words, they will probably struggle comprehending the text.

Possible modifications: Find a different, more accessible text; spend another lesson building students' understanding of vocabulary if the text is important and part of required curriculum.

Questions to Ask Yourself

▶ Do students need extra time?

▶ Do students have enough prior knowledge about the topic and genre of the complex text selection?

▶ Are context clues strong enough to use the text to determine words' meanings?

▶ Do I need to teach multiple forms of the word?

▶ Can students summarize the main points in the selection?

▶ Should I think aloud and model using context clues?

Walk around the classroom and listen to students' discussions. Note any students who aren't discussing or sharing ideas, so you know who to meet with one-on-one.

Practicing the Lessons: Second and Possibly Third Days

Circulate and listen to students' discussions. Make a note on the Vocabulary Lesson Observation form of students who aren't discussing with a partner or small group, students who consistently do not volunteer to share ideas, and those who appear to be daydreaming.

Possible modifications: Work with a pair or group and ask questions that encourage an exchange of ideas; support students who have difficulty finding situations, multiple meanings and forms, antonyms, synonyms, and the like; set aside extra time for discussions.

Questions to Ask Yourself

▶ Does the pace of instruction match students' ability to learn?

▶ Are all students contributing to discussions?

▶ Does information that specific students share show understanding?

▶ Which students ask questions that reveal confusion?

▶ Do all or a group of students need more time to understand the lesson?

▶ What do you learn about the lesson when you help individuals and pairs?

▶ What do students' comments that you've noted on chart paper or a whiteboard reveal about their understanding? Their needs?

▶ Do you need to confer with a few students to get a clearer picture of their strengths and needs?

Applying the Lessons: Completing Written Work

Review and discuss with students the directions on a reproducible. Model how you might think through a task that students will complete independently and invite students to ask questions about the task. Written work also includes students' self-evaluations and additional writing tasks completed in notebooks.

Possible modifications: Create a similar but different reproducible for ELL students and developing readers; have students complete half of the tasks; set aside 15 minutes on another day to provide extra time; work one-to-one with a student to help him or her get into completing the task.

Questions to Ask Yourself

▶ Are students following directions?

▶ How can you help students understand the directions?

▶ Do students make comments that show they understand teacher modeling?

▶ Are there students who aren't completing the reproducible? Gently ask them why. Then figure out a way to help.

▶ What does the written work tell you about students' understanding of the task?

▶ Would some or all students benefit from additional practice?

▶ What do students' self-evaluations reveal about their strengths and needs?

Self-Evaluation

When you self-reflect about the vocabulary lessons you teach, you learn how to adjust instruction in order to support students' progress with vocabulary learning. Reflection on students' behavior, questions, discussions, and written work is self-evaluation that focuses your thinking on aspects of vocabulary teaching. It enables you to understand how the lessons impacted students' learning, and it provides insights into your teaching practices. Self-evaluation can result in your modifying vocabulary lessons in four areas:

▶ Instructional methods

▶ Instructional materials

▶ Instructional time

▶ Students' tasks

Self-evaluation enables you to be a more responsive teacher as you adjust lessons to ensure students experience success and enlarge their vocabulary. Using informative assessments to effect growth in student achievement makes you a highly effective teacher (Marzano, 2012).

The outcomes of self-evaluation are the same for your students as they are for you. By self-evaluating their learning, students can observe progress and growth in enlarging their vocabulary and reading comprehension and pinpoint parts of a lesson that confuse and frustrate. Students' self-evaluations are assessments that let teachers know how much students learned and whether they require additional lessons. I've included three self-evaluations for students and a reproducible for two of them.

Exit Slips

A few minutes before the lesson ends give students a 3 × 5 index card or a slip of paper (Gere, 1985). Ask students to head the index card with their names and the date and then respond to one of these prompts that you have written on the chalkboard: *Today I learned . . . . I don't understand . . . . I need to understand ____ better. I need help with . . . . The most important thing I learned was . . . . Another lesson would help because . . . .*

Collect and read students' exit slips to gain insights into students' reactions to the lesson. Exit slips can help you decide whether students need more time, additional lessons, peer support, or can move to the next part of the lesson.

3–2–1 Strategy

At the end of a vocabulary lesson, ask students to (a) write about three things they learned or three things that were important, (b) name two words they understood better as a result of the lesson, and (c) pose one question about the lesson (Zygouris-Coe, Wiggins, & Smith, 2004). A 3–2–1 Self-Evaluation form can be found at **www.corwin.com/ vocabularyiscomprehension**.

You can adapt the 3–2–1 strategy to your needs and change what students write about. For example, I might have students write three things they didn't understand, two words that still confuse them, and one statement about how the teacher can help.

Checklist

Students can complete a checklist and then a written evaluation that responds to a specific question. You can create your own checklists.

Have students complete the Checklist for Self-Evaluating Vocabulary Learning (see **www.corwin.com/vocabularyiscomprehension**) halfway through the school year and at the end of the year. Then ask students to compare the checklist and complete a written response by noting changes and explaining why changes occurred.

How to Scaffold and Reteach

I want to clarify these terms because understanding them will help you decide whether to plan interventions that support the lesson or to reteach the lesson with a different text and vocabulary.

Scaffolding asks you to teach students in their learning zone and provide the support they need to complete a task they can't do on their own. To gradually nudge students to independence requires that you slowly release responsibility for learning to students.

Take Tessa, a sixth grader, who can't figure out situations for words independently. I plan three lessons for Tessa, each taking about 10 to 15 minutes and preferably occurring on consecutive school days. During the first lesson, I think aloud to model how I find situations for *perseverance*. First, I explain the meaning of perseverance and then tell Tessa I have to find situations where a person perseveres—doesn't give up. I suggest training for a race, practicing the piano for a recital, cleaning up an oil spill, buying food on a limited budget.

Before the second lesson starts, I explain to Tessa that I will make sure she understands the meaning of *sensitive*. I will offer two situations and ask Tessa to suggest two. Tessa can suggest only one situation: understanding a friend's feelings.

Based on Tessa's performance in the second session, I decided to continue to share the process with her using a new word. Tessa could explain the word's meaning and use an online dictionary to broaden her knowledge of the word's meanings; finding situations the word worked in was her challenge. At the next session, I modeled for Tessa that using the word to pose questions can support finding situations. For the general academic word *acquire,* I asked these questions: *What can people acquire? Why do people want to acquire things? Where can people acquire things? How does acquiring affect our minds? Our environment?* It was generating questions that jump-started Tessa into working independently.

My work with Tessa is an example of scaffolding students' learning using informative assessments to decide how much responsibility to release to her. The gradual release provides the scaffolds that can move students out of their learning zone where they are dependent on an expert for support to independence with a task. Be aware that even though students reveal progress with one set of scaffolds, at a later time, when you work on the same skill they might still require support. Our students learn by repetition, and that includes scaffolds and gradual release.

Reteaching asks teachers to prepare similar lessons using new materials and figuring out ways to teach the concept differently from the first time. Teaching the same lesson that didn't work the first time usually won't help students. Our responsibility is to reflect on why the lesson didn't work in order to make changes that can benefit students' learning. For example, a small group of sixth-grade students struggled with figuring out how repetition affected a poem's meaning. They saw repetition more as the "fa-la-la" of the chorus of a folk song even after reading and reflecting on the English ballad "Lord Randal" (see Chapter 3, pages 77–83).

I chose a simple poem, author unknown (see "August Heat," **www.corwin .com/vocabularyiscomprehension**), and asked, Why does the poet repeat "And sit" four times? First, I asked each student to read the poem out loud, saying the "And sit" the way they thought the writer intended those words to be spoken. Then students used their performances to figure out what the repetition does for the poem.

> Here's what they said: "It shows the huge heat; it shows that he [the poet] can't move any body parts; it shows that it's too hot for him to even get up."

Acting out the poem led the way to figuring out the effectiveness of repetition. Students agreed that with some poems and songs, the repetition doesn't do important work; but in many poems it does.

"August Heat"
by Anonymous

In August, when the days are hot,	1
I like to find a shady spot,	2
And hardly move a single bit—	3
And sit—	4
And sit—	5
And sit—	6
And sit!	7

Tips for Reteaching

It's definitely challenging to reteach a lesson—to find a different way to help students, but reteaching, finding a novel angle, can trigger the light of understanding. You will find ways to reteach based on your students' background and experiences and their responses to the original lesson. Here are a few suggestions to consider:

- Start by asking students, What confused you? How can I help?
- Use students' responses to frame a new lesson.
- Use new material that's accessible to students.
- Include student performance when appropriate.
- Use a graphic organizer.
- Ask students to draw their responses.
- Invite students to ask questions during the lesson.
- Use videos from TeacherTube (http://www.teachertube.com/).
- Develop learning centers for additional practice.

◆◆◆ **Collaborate and Learn** ◆◆◆

Discuss these questions/prompts with a colleague or at a faculty meeting.

1. How can informative assessment help you enable all students to expand their vocabulary?

2. What kinds of interventions have you successfully implemented? Share these with colleagues.

3. How can students' self-evaluations help you make instructional adjustments? Share and discuss some students' self-evaluations with colleagues.

4. Discuss issues surrounding finding extra time, and share the ways you've been able to set aside more time to scaffold and reteach.

Concluding Thoughts on Vocabulary Instruction

"A Word Is Dead"

by Emily Dickinson

A word is dead	1
When it is said,	2
Some say.	3
I say it just	4
Begins to live	5
That day.	6

Emily Dickinson's poem points out that speaking is one way to keep words alive. Speaking—discussions, conversations, monologues, drama, speeches—not only keeps words alive because they are used, but speaking also enables students to learn new words in diverse oral contexts. When classrooms are rich with meaningful talk and students and their teacher exchange and share ideas about content, words live.

Teachers who include vocabulary learning every day can enlarge students' knowledge of general academic and domain-specific vocabulary as well as school-task and literary words. Ten to 15 minutes a day of vocabulary instruction and learning—obsessive consistency—can develop what Beck, McKeown, and Kucan (2013) call "word consciousness." Word consciousness refers to students' awareness of and interest in words and their meanings.

However, the result is that as you improve students' vocabulary you will also be moving them closer to reading and comprehending grade-level texts (Hiebert, 2013; National Assessment of Educational Progress, 2011).

In addition to consistent vocabulary lessons, help your students understand that they can use the 10 strategies that follow to continually enlarge their thinking, speaking, reading, and writing vocabularies. You can find the list as a student handout at **www.corwin.com/vocabularyiscomprehension.**

Teachers who include vocabulary learning in their classrooms every day can broaden students' word knowledge and bring them closer to comprehending grade-level texts.

1. **Become a nonstop reader:** Read e-books, print books, blogs, and online articles. The more you read, the greater your background knowledge and the more your vocabulary will grow. Through reading, you'll meet words in diverse contexts and come to know their multiple meanings.

2. **Use new words or lose them:** Include words in your conversations, text messages, IMs, and writing. Without use, new words you've learned just fade away into the land of forgetting.

3. **Develop curiosity about multiple meanings:** When you meet a new word in one situation, take a few moments to consider its multiple meanings. Use an online dictionary or thesaurus to explore multiple meanings. Text a friend to see what he or she knows about the word.

4. **Bond with a dictionary:** If you come across an unfamiliar word, jot it on scrap paper, and when you have a free moment, read about it on an online dictionary.

5. **Play vocabulary games:** It's easy to find word games online through Google. Play games with friends, siblings, parents, and on your own. While you're having fun, you'll learn new words and revisit old friends.

6. **Broaden your interests:** Try to branch out and read beyond your interests and hobbies. Read online newspapers, take a virtual tour of a museum, castle, or city. Listen to music you love; then listen to other kinds of music. When you learn about a range of topics, you can enlarge your vocabulary.

7. **Ask questions:** If someone uses a word or expression you don't understand, ask that person to tell you about it.

8. **Talk:** Talk to friends and family; use a video chat program such as iChat to talk online; have conversations with yourself. Make talk an important part of your day, and you'll meet and learn new words that you will use as you communicate with others.

9. **Listen:** Listen during a conversation, lesson, speech, sermon, newscast, play, movie, video; listen to the words others use to convey meaning and communicate ideas. Mull over ideas and words you've heard—new words, familiar words—and discover what listening has helped you learn.

10. **Visualize words:** You can only picture, see on the screen of your mind, what you understand. Once you can use meaning and situations to picture new words, you'll be able to use them when thinking, speaking, reading, and writing.

References

Adams, M. J. (2009). The challenge of advanced tests: The interdependence of reading and learning. In E. H. Hiebert (Ed.), *Reading more, reading better?* (pp. 163–189). New York, NY: Guilford.

Afflerbach, P. (2012). *Understanding and using reading assessment, K–12* (2nd ed.). Newark, NJ: International Reading Association.

Akhavan, N. (2007). *Accelerated vocabulary instruction: Strategies for closing the achievement gap for all students*. New York, NY: Scholastic.

Allen, J. (1999). *Words, words, words: Teaching vocabulary in grades 4–12*. York, ME: Stenhouse.

Allington, R. L. (2009). If they don't read much . . . 30 years later. In E. H. Hiebert (Ed.), *Reading more, reading better* (pp. 30–54). New York, NY: Guilford.

Allington, R. L., & Gabriel, R. E. (2012). Every child, every day. *Educational Leadership, 69*(6), 10–15.

Allison, N. (2009). *Middle school readers: Helping them read widely, helping them read well*. Portsmouth, NH: Heinemann.

Baker, S. K., Simmons, D. C., & Kame'enui, E. J. (1998). Vocabulary acquisition: Research bases. In D. C. Simmons & E. J. Kame'enui (Eds.), *What reading research tells us about children with diverse learning needs: Bases and basics* (pp. 183–217). Mahwah, NJ: Erlbaum.

Baumann, J. F., & Kame'enui, E. J. (2004). *Vocabulary instruction: Research to practice*. New York, NY: Guilford.

Beals, D. (1997). Sources of support for learning words in conversation: Evidence from mealtimes. *Journal of Child Language, 24,* 673–694.

Bear, D. R., Invernizzi, M. R., Templeton, S., & Johnston, F. R. (2011). *Words their way: Word study for phonics, vocabulary, and spelling instruction* (5th ed.). New York, NY: Pearson.

Beck, I. L., McKeown, M. G., & Kucan, L. (2002). *Bringing words to life: Robust vocabulary instruction*. New York, NY: Guilford Press.

Beck, I. L., McKeown, M. G., & Kucan, L. (2013). *Bringing words to life: Robust vocabulary instruction* (2nd ed.). New York, NY: Guilford Press.

Beck, I. L., Perfetti, C. A., & McKeown, M. G. (1982). Effects of long-term vocabulary instruction on lexical access and reading comprehension. *Journal of Educational Psychology, 74*(4), 506–521.

Berne, J., & Blachowicz, C. L. Z. (2009). What reading teachers say about vocabulary instruction: Voices from the classroom. *The Reading Teacher, 62,* 314–323.

Biemiller, A. (1999). *Language and reading success*. Cambridge, MA: Brookline Books.

Biemiller, A. (2004). Teaching vocabulary in the primary grades: Vocabulary instruction needed. In J. F. Baumann & E. J. Kame'enui (Eds.), *Vocabulary instruction: Research to practice* (pp. 28–40). New York, NY: Guilford.

Biemiller, A., & Slonim, N. (2001). Estimating root word vocabulary growth in normative and advanced populations: Evidence for a common sequence of vocabulary acquisition. *Journal of Educational Psychology, 93,* 498–520.

Blachowicz, C. L. Z., & Fisher, P. J. L. (2006). *Teaching vocabulary in all classrooms*. Upper Saddle River, NJ: Pearson Education.

Blachowicz, C. L. Z., & Fisher, P. J. L. (2008). Attentional vocabulary instruction: Read-alouds, word play, and other motivating strategies for fostering informal word learning. In A. E. Farstrup & S. J. Samuels (Eds.), *What research has to say about vocabulary instruction* (pp. 32–55). Newark, DE: International Reading Association.

Blachowicz, C. L. Z., Fisher, P. J. L., Ogle, D., & Watts-Taffe, S. (2006). Vocabulary: Questions from the classroom. *Reading Research Quarterly, 41,* 524–538.

Black, P., & William, D. (1998). Assessment and classroom living. *Assessment in education: Principles, Policy, and Practice, 5*(10), 7–74.

Bravo, M. A., & Cervetti, G. N. (2008). Teaching vocabulary through text and experience in content areas. In A. E. Farstrup & S. J. Samuels (Eds.), *What research has to say about vocabulary instruction* (pp. 130–149). Newark, DE: International Reading Association.

Brozo, W. G., Shiel, G., & Topping, K. (2008). Engage in reading lessons learned from three PISA countries. *Journal of Adolescent and Adult Literacy, 51*(14), 304–315.

Burke, J. (2012). *The English teacher's companion* (4th ed.). Portsmouth, NH: Heinemann.

Chall, J. S., & Jacobs, V. A. (2003). Poor children's fourth-grade slump. *American Educator, 27*(1), 14–15, 44.

Coxhead, A. (2000). *High incidence academic word list.* http://www.cal.org/create/conferences/2012/pdfs/handout-4-vaughn-reutebuch-cortez.pdf

Cunningham, A. E. (2005). Vocabulary growth through independent reading and reading aloud to children. In E. H. Hiebert & M. L. Kamil (Eds.), *Teaching and learning vocabulary: Bringing research to practice* (pp. 45–68). Mahwah, NJ: Erlbaum.

Dunn, M., Bonner, B., & Huske, L. (2007). *Developing a systems process for improving vocabulary instruction: Lessons learned.* Retrieved from http://www.ascd.org/ASCD/pdf/Building%20Academic%20Vocabulary/Developing%20Systems%20Process.pdf

Fisher, D., Flood, J., Lapp, D., & Frey, N. (2004). Interactive read-alouds: Is there a common set of implementation practices? *The Reading Teacher, 58*(1), 8–17.

Gambrell, L. B. (1996). What research reveals about discussion. In L. B. Gambrell & J. F. Almasi (Eds.), *Lively discussions! Fostering engaged reading* (pp. 25–38). Newark, DE: International Reading Association.

Ganske, K. (2008). *Mindful of words: Spelling and vocabulary exploration 4–8.* New York, NY: Guilford.

Gere, A. R. (1985). *Roots in the sawdust: Writing to learn across the disciplines.* Urbana, IL: National Council of Teachers of English.

Giora, R. (2003). *On our mind: Salience, context, and figurative language.* New York, NY: Oxford University Press.

Glucksberg, S., & McGlone, M. S. (2001). *Understanding Figurative language: From metaphors to idioms.* New York, NY: Oxford University Press.

Gottlieb, M., & Ernst-Slavit, G. (2014). Academic language: A centerpiece for academic success in English language arts. In M. Gottlieb & G. Ernst-Slavit (Eds.), *Academic language in diverse classrooms, Grades 6–8* (pp. 1–44). Thousand Oaks, CA: Corwin.

Graham, S., & Hebert, M. A. (2010). *Writing to read: Evidence for how writing can improve reading.* New York, NY: Carnegie Corporation.

Graves, M. F. (2004). Teaching prefixes: As good as it gets? In E. J. Kame'enui & J. F. Baumann (Eds.), *Vocabulary instruction: Research to practice* (pp. 81–99). New York, NY: Guilford.

Graves, M. F. (2006). *The vocabulary book: Learning and instruction.* Newark, DE: International Reading Association.

Graves, M. F. (2008). Instruction on individual words: One size does not fit all. In A. E. Farstrup & S. J. Samuels (Eds.), *What research has to say about vocabulary instruction* (pp. 56–79). Newark, DE: International Reading Association.

Graves, M. F., Juel, C., & Graves, B. B. (1998). *Teaching reading in the 21st century.* Boston, MA: Allyn & Bacon.

Greenstein, L. (2010). *What teachers really need to know about formative assessment.* Alexandria, VA: ASCD.

Hart, B., & Risley, T. R. (2003a). The early catastrophe: The 30 million word gap. *American Educator, 27*(1), 4–9.

Hart, B., & Risley, T. R. (2003b). *Meaningful differences in the everyday experience of young American children.* Baltimore, MD: Brookes.

Heard, G. (1998). *Awakening the heart.* Portsmouth, NH: Heinemann.

Helman, L. (2008). English words needed: Creating research-based vocabulary instruction for English learners. In A. E. Farstrup & S. J. Samuels (Eds.), *What research has to say about vocabulary instruction* (pp. 183–211). Newark, DE: International Reading Association.

Hiebert, E. H. (2005). In pursuit of an effective, efficient vocabulary curriculum for elementary students. In E. H. Hiebert & M. L. Kamil (Eds.), *Teaching and learning vocabulary* (pp. 243–263). Mahwah, NJ: Erlbaum.

Hiebert, E. H. (2013). *Growing students' capacity with complex texts: Information, exposure, engagement.* TextProject & University of California, Santa Cruz. Retrieved from http://textproject.org/assets/library/powerpoints/Hiebert-webinar-Growing-Students-Capacity-with-Complex-Text-Information-Exposure-Engagement-2013-02-18.pdf

Hiebert, E. H., & Lubliner, S. (2008). The nature, learning, and instruction of general academic vocabulary. In A. E. Farstrup & S. J. Samuels (Eds.), *What research has to say about vocabulary instruction* (pp. 106–129). Newark, DE: International Reading Association.

Hoyt, L. (2013a). *Interactive read-alouds: Lesson matrix for grades 4–5.* Portsmouth, NH: Heinemann.

Hoyt, L. (2013b). *Interactive read-alouds: Lesson matrix for grades 6–7.* Portsmouth, NH: Heinemann.

Johnston, P. (2004). *Choice words: How our language affects children's learning.* York, ME: Stenhouse.

Kamil, M. L., & Hiebert, E. H. (2005). Teaching and learning vocabulary: Perspectives and persistent issues. In E. H. Hiebert & M. L. Kamil (Eds.), *Teaching and learning vocabulary: Bringing research to practice* (pp. 27–44). Mahwah, NJ: Erlbaum.

Kelley, J. G., Lesaux, N. K., Kieffer, M. J., & Faller, S. E. (2010). Effective academic vocabulary instruction in the urban middle school. *The Reading Teacher, 64*(1), 5–14.

Kieffer, M., & Lesaux, N. (2007). Breaking down words to build meaning: Morphology, vocabulary, and reading comprehension in the urban classroom. *The Reading Teacher, 61*(2), 134–144.

Kinsella, K., Stump, C. S., & Feldman, K. (2003). *Prentice Hall e-teach: Strategies for vocabulary development.* Retrieved from http://www.phschool.com/eteach/language_arts/2002_03/essay.html

Kittle, P. (2013). *Book love: Developing depth, stamina, and passion in adolescent readers.* Portsmouth, NH: Heinemann.

Krashen, S. (1993). *The power of reading: Insights from research.* Englewood, CO: Libraries Unlimited.

Larson, L., Dixon, T., & Townsend, D. (2013). How can teachers increase classroom use of academic vocabulary? *Voices From the Middle, 20*(4), 16–21.

Marzano, R. J. (2004). *Building background knowledge for academic achievement: Research for what works in schools.* Alexandria, VA: ASCD.

Marzano, R. J. (2005). *Preliminary report on the 2004–05 evaluation study of the ASCD program for building academic vocabulary.* Alexandria, VA: ASCD.

Marzano, R. J. (2009a). The art and science of teaching: Six steps to better vocabulary instruction. *Educational Leadership, 67*(1), 83–84.

Marzano, R. J. (2009b). *Formative assessment and standards-based learning.* Bloomington, IN: Marzano Research Laboratory.

Marzano, R. J. (2012). *Marzano causal teacher evaluation model: Teacher & leadership evaluation.* Retrieved from http://www.marzanocenter.com/files/WA-White-Paper-2012-04-09.pdf

Marzano, R. J., & Pickering, D. (2005). *Building academic vocabulary: Teacher's manual.* Alexandria, VA: ASCD.

Maxwell, L. A. (2013). Language demands rise with common core: New standards are accelerating the push to teach ELLs to speak "academic." *Education Week, 33*(10), S14–S16.

McKeown, M. G., Crosson, A. C., Artz, N. J., Sandora, C., & Beck, I. L. (2013). In the media: Expanding students' experience with academic vocabulary. *The Reading Teacher, 67*(1), 45–53.

Miller, D. (2009). *The book whisperer: Awakening the inner reader in every child.* Hoboken, NJ: Wiley.

Moore, D. W., & Moore, S. A. (1986). Possible sentences. In E. K. Dishner, T. W. Beans, J. E. Readence, & D. W. Moore (Eds.), *Reading in the content areas* (2nd ed., pp. 174–179). Dubuque, IA: Kendall/Hunt.

Nagy, W. E. (2005). Why vocabulary instruction needs to be long-term and comprehensive. In E. H. Hiebert & M. L. Kamil (Eds.), *Teaching and learning vocabulary: Bringing research to practice* (pp. 27–44). Mahwah, NJ: Erlbaum.

Nagy, W. E., Herman, P. A., & Anderson, R. C. (1985). Learning words from context. *Reading Research Quarterly, 20,* 233–253.

Nagy, W. E., & Hiebert, E. (2011). Toward a theory of word selection. In M. L. Kamil, P. D. Pearson, & R. Barr (Eds.), *Handbook of reading research* (Vol. 4, pp. 388–404). New York, NY: Routledge.

National Adolescent Literacy Coalition. (2007). *Foundational and emergent questions: Smart people talk about adolescent literacy.* Report by the Steering Committee of the National Adolescent Literacy Coalition. Washington, DC: Author.

National Assessment of Educational Progress. (2011). *NAEP Reading Report Card for the nation and the states.* Washington, DC: U.S. Department of Education, Office of Educational Research and Improvement.

National Assessment of Educational Progress. (2012). *NAEP, Reading Report Card for the nation and the states.* Washington, DC: U.S. Department of Education, Office of Educational Research and Improvement.

National Governors Association Center for Best Practices and the Council of Chief State School Officers. (2010). *Common Core State Standards for English, language arts & literacy in history/ social studies, science and technical subjects—Appendix A: Research supporting key elements of the standards.* Washington, DC: Author. Retrieved from http://www.corestandards.org/ assets/Appendix_A.pdf

Park, J. Y. (2013–2014). Becoming academically literate: A case study of an African immigrant youth. *Journal of Adolescent & Adult Literacy, 57*(4), 298–306.

Pearson, P. D. (2013). Research foundations of the Common Core State Standards in English language arts. In S. Neuman & L. Gambrell (Eds.), *Quality reading instruction in the age of Common Core State Standards* (pp. 237–262). Newark, DE: International Reading Association.

Rasinski, T., Padak, N., & Newton, R. M. (2008). *Greek & Latin roots: Keys to building vocabulary.* Huntington Beach, CA: Shell Education.

Rasinski, T., Padak, N., Newton, R. M., & Newton, E. (2007). *Divide, conquer, combine, and create: A vocabulary learning routine for grades 3–8.* Retrieved from http://www.timrasinski.com/ presentations/IRA07Tim_Rasinski.pdf

Robb, l. (2010). *Teaching reading in middle school: A strategic approach to teaching reading that improves comprehension and thinking.* New York, NY: Scholastic.

Robb, L. (2013). *Unlocking complex texts: A systematic framework for building adolescents' comprehension.* New York, NY: Scholastic.

Rosenberg, T. (2013). The power of talking to your baby. *New York Times*, April 10. Retrieved from http://opinionator.blogs.nytimes.com/2013/04/10/the-power-of-talking-to-your-baby

Rowe, M. L. (2008). Child-directed speech: Relation to socioeconomic status, knowledge of child development, and child vocabulary skill. *Journal of Child Language, 35*, 185–205.

Rowe, M. L. (2012). A longitudinal investigation of the role of quantity and quality of child-directed speech in vocabulary development. *Child Development, 83*, 1762–1774.

Rowe, M. L., Raudenbush, S., & Goldin-Meadow, S. (2012). The pace of vocabulary growth helps predict later vocabulary skill. *Child Development, 83*, 508–525.

Sass-Henke, A. M. (2013). Living and learning: Formative assessment in a middle level classroom. *Voices From the Middle, 21*(2), 43–47.

Scott, J., & Nagy, W. E. (2004). Developing word consciousness. In J. F. Baumann & E. J. Kame'enui (Eds.), *Vocabulary instruction: Research to practice* (pp. 201–217). New York, NY: Guilford Press.

Snow, C. E. (2013). Cold versus warm close reading: Stamina and the accumulation of misdirection. *Reading Today Online.* Retrieved from http://www.reading.org/reading-today/research/ post/lrp/2013/06/06/cold-versus-warm-close-reading-stamina-and-the-accumulation-of-misdirection#.U0Q0W1cmGGs

Stahl, S. A., & Nagy, W. E. (2006). *Teaching word meanings.* Mahwah, NJ: Erlbaum.

Tomlinson, C. A. (2007–2008). Learning to love assessment. *Educational Leadership, 65*(4), 8–13.

Tomlinson, C. A., & Cunningham, E. C. (2003). *Differentiation in practice: A resource guide for differentiating curriculum—grades 5–9.* Alexandria, VA: ASCD.

Vawter, D. H., & Costner, K. M. (2013). Differentiating instruction for ELLs. *AMLE Magazine, 1*(4), 1–12.

White, B. Y., & Frederiksen, J. R. (2000). Metacognitive facilitation: An approach to making scientific inquiry accessible to all. In J. Minstrell & E. van Zee (Eds.), *Inquiring into inquiry learning and teaching in science* (pp. 33–370). Washington, DC: American Association for the Advancement of Science.

Wormeli, R. (2007). *Differentiation: From planning to practice, grades 6–12*. York, ME: Stenhouse.

Zygouris-Coe, V., Wiggins, M. B., & Smith, L. H. (2004). Engaging students with texts: The 3–2–1 strategy. *The Reading Teacher, 58*(4), 381–384.

Literature Cited

Andersen, H. C. (1843). The nightingale. Retrieved from http://hca.gilead.org.il/nighting.html

Anonymous. (1629). Lord Randal. Retrieved from http://www.contemplator.com/child/variant 12.html

Anonymous. (1983). August heat. In L. B. Hopkins (Ed.), *The sky is full of song*. New York, NY: Harper & Row.

Blake, W. (1863). Three things to remember (excerpt from Auguries of innocence). Retrieved from http://www.public-domain-poetry.com/

Bridges, R. (1999). *Through my eyes*. New York, NY: Scholastic.

Brownwell, A. (2013). Athena and Arachne, retold. In L. Robb, *Unlocking complex texts*. New York, NY: Scholastic.

Burns, R. (1876). To a mouse, excerpt. Retrieved from http://www.public-domain-poetry.com/

Carroll, L. (1855). How doth the little crocodile. http://www.public-domain-poetry.com/

Coleridge, S. T. (1834). The rime of the ancient mariner, excerpt. Retrieved from http://www.public-domain-poetry.com

Coles, R. (2010). *The true story of Ruby Bridges*. New York, NY: Scholastic.

Dickinson, E. (1890). Because I could not stop for death. Retrieved from http://www.public-domain-poetry.com

Dickinson, E. (1862). I like to see it lap the miles. Retrieved from http://www.public-domain-poetry.com

Dickinson, E. (1890). If I can stop one heart from breaking. Retrieved from http://www.public-domain-poetry.com

Dickinson, E. (1862). I'll tell you how the sun rose. Retrieved from http://www.public-domain-poetry.com

Dickinson, E. (1858). I'm nobody. Retrieved from http://www.public-domain-poetry.com

Dickinson, E. (1896). It's all I have to bring today. Retrieved from http://www.public-domain-poetry.com

Dickinson, E. (1890). The morns are meeker than they were. Retrieved from http://www.public-domain-poetry.com

Dickinson, E. (1891). She sweeps with many-colored brooms. Retrieved from http://www.public-domain-poetry.com

Dickinson, E. (1894). There is no frigate like a book. Retrieved from http://www.public-domain-poetry.com

Dickinson, E. (1896). To make a prairie. Retrieved from http://www.public-domain-poetry.com

Dickinson, E. (1890). A train went through a burial ground. Retrieved from http://www.public-domain-poetry.com

Dickinson, E. (1894). A word is dead. Retrieved from http://www.public-domain-poetry.com

Donne, J. (1623). No man is an island. In Meditation XVII. Retrieved from http://www.public-domain-poetry.com

Douglass, F. (1845). *Narrative of the life of Frederick Douglass: An American slave*. Boston, MA: Anti-Slavery Office. Retrieved from http://www.ibiblio.org/ebooks/Douglass/Narrative/Douglass_Narrative.pdf

Eliot, G. (1874). Roses. Retrieved from http://www.public-domain-poetry.com

Emerson, R. W. (1837). Concord hymn. Retrieved from http://www.public-domain-poetry.com

Faustino, L. R. (2001). *The hickory chair*. New York, NY: Scholastic.

Field, E. (1902). The wanderer. http://www.public-domain-poetry.com

Filipovic, Z. (2006). *Zlata's diary: A child's life in wartime Sarajevo*. New York, NY: Penguin.

Freedman, R. (2008). *Freedom walkers: The story of the Montgomery bus boycott*. New York, NY: Holiday House.

Frost, R. (1916). The road not taken. Retrieved from http://www.public-domain-poetry.com

Giblin, J. C. (1997). *When plague strikes: The black death, smallpox, AIDS*. New York, NY: HarperCollins.

Goethe, J. W. von. (1782). The Erlking. Retrieved from http://talesoffaerie.blogspot .com/2010_05_01_archive.html

Hopkinson, D. (2005). *Under the quilt of night*. New York, NY: Aladdin.

Houseman, A. E. (1990). Loveliest of trees, the cherry now, In *A Shropshire lad*. New York, NY: Dover Thrift Edition. (Original work published 1896)

Hustick, L. B. (2014). *Two regions in our solar system*. Unpublished student manuscript. Winchester, VA.

Jumain, S. T. (2011). *The worst of friends: Thomas Jefferson, John Adams, and the true story of an American feud*. New York, NY: Dutton Juvenile.

Lai, T. (2013). *Inside out & back again*. New York, NY: HarperCollins.

Lee, M. (2006). *Landed*. New York, NY: Farrar, Straus & Giroux.

Lincoln, A. (1863). The Gettysburg address. Retrieved from https://archive.org/stream/gettys burgaddres00linc/gettysburgaddres00linc_djvu.txt

Lindsey, V. (1916). The empty boats. Retrieved from http://www.public-domain-poetry.com

Lockhart, J. A. (2013). *Horrible Henry* (excerpt). Unpublished student manuscript. Winchester, VA.

Longfellow, H. W. (1847). *Evangeline: A tale of Acadie* (excerpt). Retrieved from http://utc.iath .virginia.edu/sentimnt/evanhp.html

Longfellow, H. W. (1840). The village blacksmith. Retrieved from http://www.public-domain-poetry.com

Marin, A. (2012). *Years of dust: The story of the Dust Bowl*. New York, NY: Puffin.

Martel, L. (2003). *Life of Pi*. New York, NY: Mariner Books.

Masefield, J. (1916). Sea fever. Retrieved from http://www.public-domain-poetry.com

Miller, D. S. (2012). *Survival at 40 below*. New York, NY: Walker.

Miller, W. (1997). *Richard Wright and the library card*. New York, NY: Lee & Low.

Morris, G. P. (1837). Woodman spare that tree! Retrieved from http://www.public-domain-poetry.com

Murphy, J. (2000). *Blizzard!* New York, NY: Scholastic.

Murphy, J. (2010). *The great fire*. New York, NY: Scholastic.

Naylor, P. R. (2000). *Shiloh*. New York, NY: Aladdin.

Northup, S. (1841–1853). *Twelve years a slave: Narrative of Solomon Northup, a citizen of New-York, kidnapped in Washington City in 1841 and rescued in 1853* (excerpt). Retrieved from http://docsouth.unc.edu/fpn/northup/northup.html

Noyes, A. (1913). The highwayman (excerpt). Retrieved from http://www.potw.org/archive/potw85.html

Park, L. S. (2011). *A long walk to water: Based on a true story*. Boston, MA: HMH Books for Young Readers.

Paterson, K. (2004). *Lyddie*. New York, NY: Puffin.

Paulsen, G. (2006). *Hatchet*. New York, NY: Simon & Shuster.

Pennypacker, N. (2009). *Sparrow girl*. New York, NY: Disney-Hyperion.

Poe, E. A. (1849). The bells (excerpt). Retrieved from http://www.public-domain-poetry.com

Poe, E. A. (1845). The raven (excerpt). Retrieved from http://www.public-domain-poetry.com

Robb, A. (2014). Bedtime. Unpublished manuscript. Winchester, VA.

Robb, A. (2014). Forecast. Unpublished manuscript. Winchester, VA.

Robb, A. (2014). Frost. Unpublished manuscript. Winchester, VA.

Rossetti, C. G. (1866). A chill. Retrieved from http://www.public-domain-poetry.com

Rossetti, C. G. (2012). A diamond or a coal. Retrieved from http://www.poemhunter.com/i/ebooks/pdf/christina_georgina_rossetti_2012_3.pdf (Original work published 1879)

Rossetti, C. G. (1882). Expressions. Retrieved from http://www.public-domain-poetry.com

Rossetti, C. G. (1893). Flint. *Sing-song: A nursery rhyme book*. New York, NY: Macmillan.

Rossetti, C. G. (1893). O wind why do you never rest. *Sing-song: A nursery rhyme book*. New York, NY: Macmillan.

Rossetti, C. G. (1893). Who has seen the wind? *Sing-song: A nursery rhyme book*. New York, NY: Macmillan.

Sandburg, C. (1919). Fog. In L. Untermeyer (Ed.), *Modern American poetry*. New York, NY: Harcourt, Brace and Howe.

Sanger, G. P. (1866). *Public resolution transcribed from the thirty-ninth congress, Session I, Resolution 11: Statutes at large, treaties, and proclamations, of the United States of America* (Vol. 19). Boston, MA: Little, Brown.

Sewell, A. (2003). *Black Beauty*. New York, NY: Scholastic Classics. (Original work published 1877)

Shakespeare, W. (1600). Fairy's song. In *A midsummer night's dream*, act II, scene 2. Retrieved from http://www.poemhunter.com/poem/a-fairy-song

Shakespeare, W. (1597). O serpent heart (excerpt). In *Romeo and Juliet*, Act 3, Scene 2. Retrieved from http://poetry.rapgenius.com/William-shakespeare-romeo-and-juliet-act-3-scene-2-annotated#note-3008262

Shakespeare, W. (1983). Song of the witches. *Macbeth*. In *The Random House book of poetry for children*. New York, NY: Random House. (Original work published 1606)

Stevenson, R. L. (2008). The land of counterpane. In *A child's garden of verses*. Retrieved from http://www.gutenberg.org/files/25610/25610-h/25610-h.htm (Original work published 1885)

Stevenson, R. L. (2008). Windy nights. In *A child's garden of verses*. Retrieved from http://www.gutenberg.org/files/25610/25610-h/25610-h.htm (Original work published 1885)

Talbot, H. (2000). *Forging freedom: A true story of the Holocaust*. New York, NY: Putnam.

Taylor, M. (1998). *The friendship*. New York, NY: Puffin.

Taylor, M. (1998). *The gold Cadillac*. New York, NY: Puffin.

Teasdale, S. (1915). A fantasy. Retrieved from http://www.public-domain-poetry.com

Teasdale, S. (1911). The kind moon. Retrieved from http://www.public-domain-poetry.com

Tennyson, A. L. (1851). The eagle. Retrieved from http://www.public-domain-poetry.com

Tennyson, A. L. (1883). The owl. Retrieved from http://www.public-domain-poetry.com

Tolstoy, L. (1872). The king and the shirt. Retrieved from http://ulyssescastillo.blogspot.com/2007/08/leo-tolstoys-fables.html

Tolstoy, L. (1872). The two brothers. Retrieved from http://northwestgreatbooks.org/startup_reading.pdf

Truth, S. (1851). Ain't I a woman? Retrieved from https://www.nolo.com/legal-encyclopedia/content/truth-woman-speech.html

Watkins, Y. K. (2008). *So far from the bamboo grove*. New York, NY: HarperCollins.

Whitman, W. (1865). O captain, my captain. Retrieved from http://www.public-domain-poetry.com

Wilde, O. (1906). *The Canterville ghost* (excerpt). Retrieved from http://www.eastoftheweb.com/short-stories/UBooks/CanGho.shtml

Wordsworth, W. (1807). I wandered lonely as a cloud. Retrieved from http://www.public-domain-poetry.com

Yeats, W. B. (1890). The lake isle of Innisfree. Retrieved from http://www.public-domain-poetry.com

Yoo, P. (2005). *Sixteen years in sixteen seconds: The Sammy Lee story*. New York, NY: Lee & Low.

Index

BECAUSE ALL TEACHERS ARE LEADERS

CORWIN

A SAGE Company

Corwin is committed to improving education for all learners by publishing books and other professional development resources for those serving the field of PreK–12 education. By providing practical, hands-on materials, Corwin continues to carry out the promise of its motto: **"Helping Educators Do Their Work Better."**